Max
Alioth

Architekt
Zeichner
Wegbereiter

Max Alioth

Architect
Draughtsman
Trailblazer

Herausgegeben von / Edited by
Beat Keusch, Ulrike Jehle-Schulte Strathaus

Mit Texten von / With contributions by
Roger Diener, Ulrike Jehle-Schulte Strathaus,
Vincent Melilli, Andreas Ruby
und mit Fotografien von / and with photographs by
Serge Hasenböhler, Christian Vogt

Scheidegger & Spiess

Vorwort	6
«... und Architektur *ist* eine Kunst!» *Ulrike Jehle-Schulte Strathaus*	8
Max Alioth und das Schweizerische Architekturmuseum S AM *Roger Diener*	14
Ceci n'est pas un musée d'architecture. Über das Vermächtnis von Max Alioth *Andreas Ruby*	20
Ausgewählte Bauten	33
Die Kunsthochschule von Max Alioth und Susanna Biedermann in Marrakesch *Vincent Melilli*	120
Skizzen, Zeichnungen und Aquarelle	127
Städte und Landschaften *Ulrike Jehle-Schulte Strathaus*	158
Werkverzeichnis	163

Foreword	7
"...and, by the way, architecture *is* an artform!" Ulrike Jehle-Schulte Strathaus	9
Max Alioth and the Swiss Architecture Museum S AM Roger Diener	15
Ceci n'est pas un musée d'architecture. The legacy of Max Alioth Andreas Ruby	21
Selected buildings	33
Max Alioth and Susanna Biedermann's School of Visual Arts in Marrakech Vincent Melilli	121
Sketches, drawings, and watercolours	127
Cities and landscapes Ulrike Jehle-Schulte Strathaus	159
Catalogue of works	163

Wenn wir mit diesem Buch an Max Alioth (1930–2010) erinnern, so rücken wir für einmal eine Persönlichkeit ins Licht der Öffentlichkeit, die diese selbst nie gesucht hatte. Weder als Architekt noch als unermüdlich zeichnender Beobachter, und erst recht nicht als Förderer und Gönner drängte sich Alioth in den Vordergrund. Zu wichtig war ihm die Sache selbst: ein Bauwerk, eine Landschaft oder eine öffentliche kulturelle Einrichtung, der er als *spiritus rector* auf die Beine helfen konnte. Aus dem Architekturmuseum in Basel ist schliesslich das Schweizerische Architekturmuseum geworden, und in Marrakesch wird mit der École Supérieure des Arts Visuels (ÉSAV) ‹Afrikas beste Filmschule› betrieben – das ist nicht zuletzt Max Alioths Verdienst.

Wir danken allen, die uns bei der Verwirklichung dieses Buches unterstützt haben, mit Rat und Tat, und auch dies – ganz im Sinne von Max Alioth – ohne viel Aufhebens.

In commemorating Max Alioth (1930–2010) with this book, we are for focusing on a personality who never sought the limelight himself. Neither in his role as architect nor as a tireless observer and draughtsman, and certainly not as a patron and sponsor, did Alioth ever try to steal the show. For him, attention was always on the issue itself: a building, a landscape, or a cultural institution he was able to get off the ground in his role as guiding spirit. The Museum of Architecture in Basel eventually became the Swiss Architecture Museum, and, in Marrakech, the École Supérieure des Arts Visuels (ÉSAV) grew to become "Africa's best film school" – not least thanks to Max Alioth.

We wish to thank all those who helped us to realize this book, either with words or with deeds and – again absolutely in Max Alioth's spirit – without much ado.

«... und Architektur *ist* eine Kunst!»

Ulrike Jehle-Schulte Strathaus

Unmittelbar nach dem Zweiten Weltkrieg hat Max Alioth seine Lehre als Hochbauzeichner im Büro von Ernst Egeler angetreten und damit einen Weg eingeschlagen, der über die praktische, baunahe Ausbildung zur Architektur führt. Egeler (1908–1978) galt im Kreis der Basler Architekten des Neuen Bauens als Macher, der Hannes Meyer ans Bauhaus nach Dessau folgte, als dieser dort in den letzten Lebensjahren der Schule die Architektur wieder näher ans Bauen heranführen wollte. Wenig später gehörte Egeler zu jenen Künstlern und Bauschaffenden, die in Basel als ‹Gruppe 33› die Avantgarde vertraten.

In dieser Spanne von Bauen, Architektur und bildender Kunst fand der junge Max Alioth ein anregendes Milieu, in dem die Architektur in jedem Sinne weit gedacht und gelebt wurde. Kein Wunder zog es ihn nach 1952 ins Ausland, wo er jeweils in ausgewählten renommierten Büros arbeitete: in Paris bei Beaudouin und Lods, in Brüssel bei Egon Eiermann (Expo 1958, deutscher Pavillon, mit Sep Ruf), in München bei Alexander von Branca. Zurück in Basel, arbeitete er zunächst 1958/1959 im Büro von Förderer, Otto, Zwimpfer und von 1960 bis 1967 auch wieder bei Ernst Egeler.

Max Alioth in seinem Atelier im Klingental, Basel   Max Alioth in his studio in the Klingental, Basel

"... and, by the way, architecture *is* an artform!"

Ulrike Jehle-Schulte Strathaus

Immediately after the Second World War, Max Alioth began his apprenticeship as a structural draughtsman at the office of Ernst Egeler, thus embarking on a path that led him to architecture by way of a very practical and construction-oriented training. Among the followers of Modernist Architecture in Basel, Ernst Egeler (1908–1978) was regarded as a man of action. He followed Hannes Meyer to the Bauhaus in Dessau when the latter attempted to bring architecture back closer to actual construction during the last years of the famous school's life. Shortly afterwards, Egeler joined the group of avantgarde artists and architects in Basel, who became known as "Group 33".

In this creative world bridging construction, architecture, and visual art, young Max Alioth found a stimulating milieu, an environment in which architecture was thought and lived in a very broad sense. Not surprisingly, he moved abroad after 1952 where he worked for various renowned architectural offices: for Beaudouin and Lods in Paris, for Egon Eiermann (Expo 1958, German pavilion, with Sep Ruf) in Brussels, and for Alexander von Branca in Munich. Back in Basel, he was employed at the office of Förderer, Otto, Zwimpfer from 1958–1959 before going back to Ernst Egeler for whom he worked from 1960 to 1967.

At roughly the age of 30, he built a house for himself in Reinach which immediately attracted attention in professional circles, and, in hindsight, bore a number of programmatic features including the constructive discipline that hallmarks the ideals of Modernist Architecture as well as a few intriguing new impulses from Scandinavia and the USA.

Im Alter von rund 30 Jahren baute er sich ein eigenes Haus in Reinach, das in Fachkreisen sogleich Aufmerksamkeit fand und in der Rückschau programmatische Züge erhält: Die Verankerung in den Idealen des Neuen Bauens ist in der konstruktiven Disziplin ebenso unverkennbar wie die Anziehungskraft der neuen Impulse aus Skandinavien oder den USA. 1968 schloss Alioth sich mit Urs Remund (1928–2012) zu einer Arbeitsgemeinschaft zusammen. Mit ihren rund 30 Wettbewerbsbeiträgen, einer Vielzahl von Bauten und dem Einsatz in den Fachverbänden (BSA 1973) waren Alioth und Remund bis in die 1990er Jahre eine feste Grösse im Architekturleben in Basel.

Von Anfang an waren Zeichenstift und Aquarellkasten Alioths ständige Begleiter, auch auf den vielen Reisen, die er unternahm. Eine Tradition, die schon sein im Engadin tätiger Onkel gleichen Namens hervorragend gepflegt hatte, setzte er so fort. 1981 waren einige seiner Arbeiten in einer Ausstellung in der Galerie ‹zem Specht› in Basel zu sehen.

Max Alioth (l.) und Urs Remund (r.) anlässlich der Neueröffnung des Antikenmuseums Basel und Sammlung Ludwig, 1988

Max Alioth (l.) and Urs Remund (r.) at the opening of the Antikenmuseum Basel und Sammlung Ludwig, 1988

In 1968 Alioth joined forces with Urs Remund (1928–2012) to form a working partnership. With their roughly 30 competition entries, an impressive number of buildings, and their dedicated involvement in professional associations (BSA 1973), Alioth and Remund became firmly established players in Basel's architectural world well into the 1990s.

From the start, his drawing kit and a box of watercolours were Alioth's steady companions, not least on his many journeys, thus continuing a tradition his uncle by the same name had previously already cultivated during his work in the Engadin. In 1981, a selection of Alioth's works were shown in an exhibition at the gallery "zem Specht" in Basel.

Max Alioth verstand seine Aufgabe immer auch in einem weiteren Sinne als kulturelle Verpflichtung und engagierte sich in verschiedenen Institutionen. Die bedeutsamsten sind die Stiftung Schweizerisches Architekturmuseum in Basel, die er 1984 mitbegründete, und der Aufbau des Kulturhauses Dar Bellarj und der École Supérieure des Arts Visuels ÉSAV in Marrakesch, die er zusammen mit und angeregt durch seine Frau Susanna Biedermann als kulturellen Beitrag für kommende Generationen in Marokko 1998 eingerichtet und fortan grosszügig unterstützt hatte.

Max Alioth und Susanna Biedermann in ihrem Wohnhaus ‹Haus für zwei› in Basel

Max Alioth am Zeichentisch in Marrakesch mit Vincent Melilli, dem zukünftigen Direktor der ÉSAV

Vincent Melilli, Prince Moulay Rachid, Martin Scorsese und Max Alioth während der Einweihung der ÉSAV, am 12. Dezember 2007

Max Alioth and Susanna Biedermann at their home "Haus für zwei" in Basel

Max Alioth at his drawing board in Marrakech with Vincent Melilli, the later director of the ÉSAV

Vincent Melilli, Prince Moulay Rachid, Martin Scorsese, and Max Alioth at the opening of the ÉSAV on 12 December 2007

Throughout, Max Alioth considered his work as a kind of cultural commitment in the wider sense of the term. Accordingly, he was involved in various institutions, the most significant being the Swiss Architecture Museum Foundation in Basel, which he co-founded in 1984, and the cultural centre Dar Bellarj along with the École Supérieure des Arts Visuels ÉSAV in Marrakech, which he set up together with, and inspired by, his wife Susanna Biedermann in the sense of a cultural contribution to Morocco's future generations in 1998 and which he continued to support generously.

The text is based on two articles by Ulrike Jehle-Schulte Strathaus: Obituary in Basler Zeitung of 24 April 2010, p. 34; idem "Hoher Durschnitt", Fragen zur Archivierung von Architekturnachlässen der Spätmoderne, in: Forum Stadt 42, 2015, 1, pp. 79–82. The quotation in the title is from Max Alioth, in: Architektur-Wettbewerb, Beitrag zur Entwicklung, in: Hochbauamt Basel-Stadt: Projekte für Basel, Architektur-Wettbewerbe 1979–1983. Basel 1983, pp. 47, 48; emphasis by the editor.

Max Alioth und das Schweizerische Architekturmuseum

Roger Diener

Viele haben zur Eröffnung des Architekturmuseums in Basel beigetragen, aber gegründet hat es Max Alioth, zusammen mit Ulrike und Werner Jehle. Ulrike und Werner hatten die Idee zum Museum und sie hatten erfahren, dass das Domus-Haus, ein selten wertvolles Baudenkmal der Nachkriegsmoderne der 50er Jahre, verkauft werden sollte. Max, ein hochkultivierter Architekt, um dessen professionelle Unbestechlichkeit alle wussten, die in irgendeiner Weise mit Entwerfen und Produzieren von Architektur zu tun hatten, war bereits der grandiose Ambassador dieses Museums, als es erst eine Idee war.

Ulrike, Werner und Max bildeten ein schlagkräftiges Team, es verkörperte Forschung, Lehre, Theorie und Praxis von Architektur beispielhaft. Sie waren sich im Schweizerischen Werkbund bereits früher begegnet und hatten sich unter anderem für den Erhalt schützenswerter Bauwerke verwendet. Sie haben meinen Vater und mich ins Boot geholt. Die Hürde war hoch, der Preis für das Haus in dieser Zeit des boomenden Detailhandels war an der oberen Grenze des Immobilienmarktes angesetzt. Innert weniger Wochen sollte das Geld für das Haus aufgebracht werden. Eine Aktiengesellschaft, um das Haus zu erwerben, und eine Stiftung,

Max Alioth und Ulrike Jehle-Schulte Strathaus bei der Eröffnung der Ausstellung ‹Räume wie Stilleben› am 3. Dezember 1994

Max Alioth and Ulrike Jehle-Schulte Strathaus at the opening of the exhibition *Räume wie Stilleben* on 3 December 1994

Max Alioth and the Swiss Architecture Museum

Roger Diener

Many people were involved in the opening of the Architecture Museum in Basel, but it was Max Alioth who actually founded it together with Ulrike and Werner Jehle. Ulrike and Werner were already thinking along these lines when they heard that the Domus House, an architectural jewel of 1950s post-war modernism, was up for sale. Max, a highly accomplished architect, whose professional integrity was well known to people involved in designing and producing architecture, already featured as the museum's grand ambassador when it was still merely an idea.

Ulrike, Werner, and Max formed a powerful team, representing architectural research, teaching, theory, and practice in a copybook manner. They had met through the Swiss Werkbund, an association of artists, designers, and architects, and had already previously lobbied for the preservation of valuable historic buildings. It was then that they also brought me and my father on board. The stakes were high, since, given the economic boom at the time, the price for the Domus House was at the upper limit of the real estate market. Moreover, the money for the house had to be raised within a few weeks. They decided to set up a joint-stock company to purchase the house, and a foundation to run the museum, with Max Alioth as chairman of the foundation.

Architects and local building companies were asked to follow the initiators' example and acquire shares in the new company, and, hey presto, the unlikely came true: the initiators were able to acquire the Domus House, which provided space for the museum across five floors. Hence, the house was preserved in its original shell and structure; a sale on the open market would have probably ended in an extensive and ruthless refurbishment of the old structure.

In a calm manner and a clear voice, Max Alioth championed the cause of the museum within and beyond the local architectural

um das Museum zu betreiben, sollten gegründet werden. Max Alioth sollte das Präsidium der Stiftung übernehmen.

Architekten und Firmen des Baugewerbes wurden darum gebeten, es den Initianten gleichzutun und Anteilscheine der Aktiengesellschaft zu übernehmen. Schliesslich wurde das Unwahrscheinliche Realität: Das Domus-Haus konnte erworben werden und bot dem Architekturmuseum auf fünf Geschossen Raum. Das Haus konnte so auch in seiner originalen Struktur und Hülle erhalten werden; bei einem Verkauf am Immobilienmarkt hätte eine zerstörerische Erneuerung des Hauses gedroht.

Unaufgeregt und mit heller Stimme hat Max Alioth die Sache des Museums in- und ausserhalb der Architektenszene vorgebracht. Er hat die traditionelle Grenze zwischen jenen Architekten, die sich als Vertreter der Disziplin mit grossem ‹A› geschrieben wähnen, und den Entwicklern und Baugewerblern nicht nur überwunden, sondern aufgelöst und sie, zusammen mit Gleichgesinnten, in diesem Konstrukt von Stiftung und Aktiengesellschaft zusammengeführt. Viele waren dazu bereit, gleichzuziehen und das Museum mit ihrem Einsatz zu ermöglichen. Für die fehlenden 2 Millionen Franken wurde eine Hypothek aufgenommen.

1984 erfolgte schliesslich die glamouröse Eröffnung des Architekturmuseums mit der atemberaubenden Installation des Künstlerpaars Jeanne-Claude und Christo. Max Alioth schenkte seine ganze Aufmerksamkeit dem Auftrag des Hauses, Architektur zu vermitteln. Ulrike und Max bildeten ein kongeniales Team. Erstaunliches haben sie zustandegebracht. Als Präsident hat Max die Geschicke des Museums mit grösster Aufmerksamkeit gelenkt. Sein Ausdruck während der zahlreichen Sitzungen des Stiftungsrats hat sich nie gewandelt. Hellwach und präzise hat er zugehört und argumentiert, zugleich stand ihm das Wohlwollen ins Gesicht geschrieben. Max, so kam es mir immer vor, wurde gleichermassen von seinem kritischen Verstand wie von seiner immensen Zuneigung zu unserem Auftrag getrieben – meist mit einem feinen Lächeln getarnt. Es galt immer wieder, schwierige Situationen zu meistern; wiederholt

scene. He not only overcame the traditional boundary between those architects who regarded themselves as representatives of a discipline spelt with a capital "A", and normal developers and constructors, he actually erased the boundary and brought everybody together as one under the umbrella of the foundation and joint-stock company. Many of them were prepared to follow suit and make the museum come true through their commitment. The outstanding two million franks were covered by a mortgage.

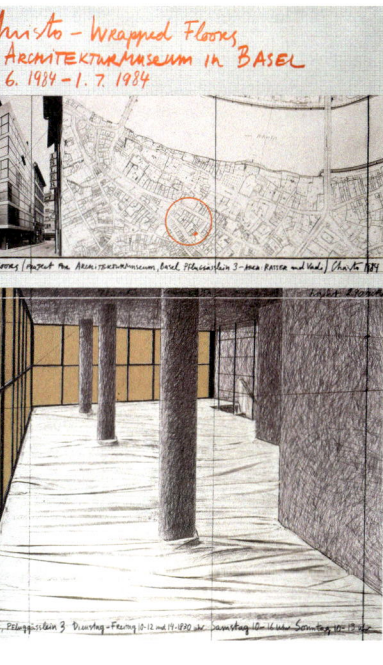

Finally, in 1984, the Architecture Museum had its grand opening with a breathtaking installation by the artist couple Jeanne-Claude and Christo. Max Alioth devoted his entire time and attention to the museum's stated mission, namely to convey and explain architecture. Ulrike and Max were a congenial team and achieved amazing things. In his role as chairman, Max steered the fortunes of the museum with great care and dedication. During the many meetings of the foundation's Board of Trustees, the expression on his face never changed. He was a keen listener and argued his point with acute conviction, but always with an air of good will

Christo and Jeanne-Claude, *Wrapped floors* in the Domus House on the occasion of the opening of the Architecture Museum in Basel on 15 June 1984

liessen konjunkturelle Krisen des Baugewerbes sichere Geldquellen plötzlich versiegen. Wenn gar nichts mehr half, hat Max uns Stiftungsräte in die Pflicht genommen, jederzeit, wie schon für die Gründung des Museums, selbst voranschreitend. Seine ungeschönte, realistische Einschätzung der schwierigen ökonomischen Aspekte, verbunden mit seiner Liebe für das Architekturmuseum, bildeten ein feingliedriges und dennoch unzerstörbares Bollwerk.

2004 eröffnete sich im Rahmen einer Umgestaltung die Möglichkeit für das Architekturmuseum, in der Kunsthalle Basel neue Ausstellungsräume zu mieten. Parallel bewarb sich das Museum um den Titel ‹Schweizerisches Architekturmuseum›. Wäre beides erreicht, wollte Max Alioth das Präsidium der Stiftung weitergeben und Ulrike Jehle wollte das Museum am neuen Domizil noch einführen, um es danach in neue Hände zu legen. Zuvor bedurfte es allerdings ähnlich grosser ökonomischer Anstrengungen wie jene zur Gründung des Museums. Die Aktionäre des Domus-Hauses sollten ihre Anteile, ohne entschädigt zu werden, der Stiftung des Architekturmuseums überlassen. Das ist unter der Führung von Max Alioth, der selbst mit dem Beispiel voranging, schliesslich gelungen. Damit das Schweizerische Architekturmuseum ohne ökonomische Altlasten neu lanciert werden konnte, galt es, die beträchtliche Hypothek des Domus-Hauses abzulösen – eine nicht zu bewältigende Aufgabe. Ich erinnere mich an die Ratlosigkeit im Stiftungsrat und das betroffene Schweigen. Da sagte Max ganz ruhig, dass er das bereits selbst besorgt hätte. Ohne Max Alioth wäre das Architekturmuseum in Basel 1984 im Domus-Haus nicht gegründet worden und ohne ihn wäre die Institution 2006 nicht zum Schweizerischen Architekturmuseum in der Kunsthalle Basel geworden.

and friendliness written across his face. The impression I always got was that Max was driven in equal measure by his critical mind and his love for the cause – most of the time behind a gentle smile. Time and again, we had to master difficult situations, especially when our financial resources threatened to run dry during one of the many recurrent crises in the building industry. When nothing else helped, Max would take the board members up on their promise but not without himself setting the example, as he had done when the museum was born. His plain-spoken, realistic assessment of a difficult economic situation in combination with his love for the museum, formed a delicate yet insurmountable bastion.

In 2004, in the context of a redesign, the opportunity arose for the museum to move to new premises in the Kunsthalle Basel. At the same time, the museum applied for the right to call itself Swiss Architecture Museum. As soon as both goals had been achieved, Max Alioth wanted to step down as chairman of the foundation while Ulrike Jehle was prepared to remain on until the museum was up and running at its new location, before handing the reigns to a new pair of hands. Before that could happen, similarly great economic efforts were required as at the time the museum was founded. The shareholders of the Domus House were asked to forfeit their shares, without compensation, to the Architecture Museum Foundation. Under the guidance of Max Alioth, who led by example, this was finally accomplished. In order for the new Swiss Architecture Museum to be launched without being burdened by financial liabilities, the sizeable mortgage had to be paid off – to tell the truth, an impossible task. I well remember the board members' prolonged silence and long faces when they were given the news – until Max Alioth said in a calm voice that he had already taken care of the problem! Without Max Alioth, the Architecture Museum in the Domus House in Basel would never have seen the light of day in 1984, and without him the institution would never have become the Swiss Architecture Museum at the Kunsthalle Basel twenty-two years later.

Ceci n'est pas un musée d'architecture.
Über das Vermächtnis von Max Alioth

Andreas Ruby

Max Alioth war und ist für das Schweizerische Architekturmuseum eine Persönlichkeit von überragender Bedeutung. Als Initiator, Gründer und grosszügiger Stifter des Museums verkörpert er bis heute ein leuchtendes Beispiel für die elementare Bedeutung zivilgesellschaftlichen Engagements für die Kultur in der Schweiz. Er war ein exemplarischer Vertreter jener kulturellen Existenzgründer, die durch ihr ebenso entschiedenes wie uneigennütziges Wirken den Grundstein für die aussergewöhnliche Qualität des kulturellen Lebens in der Schweiz gelegt haben. Denn während in Ländern wie Frankreich oder Deutschland die Institutionenbildung der Kultur primär eine Angelegenheit des Staates ist, gehen viele kulturelle Institutionen in der Schweiz originär auf das Wirken von Privatpersonen zurück. Dies zeigt sich besonders auf dem Gebiet der Museen. In der Schweiz gibt es über tausend Museen. Mehr als die Hälfte davon wurde von privaten Trägern gegründet. Auslöser dafür waren oft eine oder mehrere Persönlichkeiten, die der Überzeugung waren, dass ein bestimmtes Thema ein Museum so sehr brauche, dass man nicht darauf warten solle, bis der Staat diese Notwendigkeit realisiert. Das Schweizerische Architekturmuseum ist ein Museum, das genau auf diese Weise entstanden ist.

    Aber das Schweizerische Architekturmuseum verdankt Max Alioth noch mehr als seine Existenz. Es verdankt ihm auch seine ureigene Identität. Denn durch die Entscheidung, die Gründung des Museums 1984 mit der Rettung eines wichtigen Gebäudes der Basler Nachkriegsmoderne, des 1958 von Rasser und Vadi gebauten Domus-Haus, zu verknüpfen, erhielt das Museum ein programmatisches Fundament, das es von allen bekannten Architekturmuseen unterscheiden sollte und seine Entwicklung bis heute prägt. Das Domus-Haus stand damals leer und sollte verkauft werden, und es war zu befürchten, dass es dabei architektonisch entstellt

Ceci n'est pas un musée d'architecture. The legacy of Max Alioth

Andreas Ruby

Max Alioth was and still is a personality of outstanding importance for the Swiss Architecture Museum. In his role as the museum's initiator, founder, and generous sponsor, he remains a beacon of elementary relevance regarding the commitment by civil society to the arts and culture in Switzerland. He was an exemplary representative of those cultural entrepreneurs who, through their equally resolute and selfless commitment, helped to lay the foundations for the exceptional quality of cultural life in Switzerland. While in countries such as France or Germany, the establishment of cultural institutions is primarily a matter for the state, many cultural facilities in Switzerland owe their existence to the determined initiative of private individuals. This is especially the case where museums are concerned. In Switzerland there are more than a thousand museums; over half of them were founded by private sponsors, often prompted by one or several personalities who felt that a certain topic needed a museum so much that they couldn't wait for the state to become active in this respect. The Swiss Architecture Museum is a good example at hand.

However, the Swiss Architecture Museum owes much more to Max Alioth than its mere existence. It owes him its very identity. For the decision to wed the founding of the museum in 1984 with the preservation of a significant building of Basel's post-war modernism – the Domus House built by Rasser and Vadi in 1958 – lent the museum a programmatic foundation that not only distinguished it from all other well-known architectural museums, but actually informs its development to this day. Back then, the Domus House stood deserted and was up for sale, and if that had gone ahead, the danger of the building's architectural disfigurement loomed ahead. The fact that Max Alioth appeared on the scene at that moment and began rallying architects and contractors to purchase the building

werden würde. Dass Max Alioth in dieser Situation auf den Plan trat und Architekten und Bauunternehmer dafür zu mobilisieren vermochte, das Haus kollektiv zu erwerben, um ihm dieses Schicksal zu ersparen, ist ein ungewöhnliches und faszinierendes Gründungsnarrativ für ein Architekturmuseum. Denn es versinnbildlicht ein sehr besonderes Museumsverständnis, in dem das Gebäude nicht einfach nur das bauliche Behältnis des Museums ist, sondern auch sein einziges, sein eigentliches Exponat.

Mit dieser Identifikation von Idee und Körper erinnert das Projekt des Architekturmuseums in Basel an das fast gleichzeitig entstandene Deutsche Architekturmuseum in Frankfurt. Doch während für Letzteres eine repräsentative gründerzeitliche Villa stark umgebaut wurde, die in ihrem Bestand nicht gefährdet war, sondern sich aufgrund ihrer Lage am Schaumainkai dafür anbot, Teil der geplanten Museumsmeile zu werden, war die Transformation des Domus-Hauses zum Architekturmuseum eine bewusste Rettungstat für eine bedrohte Architektur, die damals von der Gesellschaft nicht als schützenswert betrachtet wurde. Auch der architektonische Umgang mit den Bestandsbauten ist in beiden Fällen sehr unterschiedlich. Der Bau des Deutschen Architekturmuseums von Oswald Mathias Ungers ist im Wesentlichen ein Neubau innerhalb der stehengelassenen Aussenwände der Villa von 1912; es ist die bauliche Collage aus Alt und Neu, die das Museum zur Ikone der architektonischen Postmoderne werden liess. Das Domus-Haus in Basel wurde dagegen in Gänze erhalten und von Roger Diener nur minimal und behutsam für den Ausstellungsbetrieb adaptiert. Die architektonischen Botschaften der beiden Gebäude unterscheiden sich also deutlich. Während das Museum in Frankfurt die Postmoderne als architekturhistorischen Brückenschlag von der Vergangenheit in die Gegenwart zelebriert (und die Moderne dabei diskret überspringt), ging es den Museumsgründern in Basel um Max Alioth darum, einem existenziell bedrohten Vertreter einer wenig geliebten Moderne durch eine neue Nutzung ein zweites Leben zu schenken. Das Projekt des Archi-

as a collective in order to spare it this fate, is an unusual and fascinating founding narrative for a museum of architecture. For it signifies a very special understanding of a museum in which the building serves not merely as an architectural shell but actually as the museum's only, its actual exhibit.

This alignment of idea and body in the case of the architecture museum in Basel calls to mind the German Museum of Architecture DAM in Frankfurt, which was established at around the same time. While in the latter case a representative mansion dating from the Gründerzeit whose existence was not endangered but, instead, lent itself to becoming part of the planned museum mile due to its location on Schaumainkai was substantially remodelled, the transformation of the Domus House into an architectural museum represents a conscious act of saving a building, which the Basel public did not deem worthy of protection at the time. The way the two existing buildings were dealt with in architectural terms also differs strongly. The building of the German Museum of Architecture by Oswald Mathias Ungers is basically a new structure raised within the old mansion's outer walls of 1912; it represents a structural collage of new and old which makes the museum an icon of postmodern architecture. The Domus House in Basel, on the other hand, was preserved in its entirety and only minimally and cautiously adapted by Roger Diener to serve as an exhibition space. Thus, the architectural messages communicated by the two buildings differ markedly. While the Frankfurt museum celebrates postmodernism as an architectural-historical bridge between past and present (quietly by-passing modernism in the process), the initiators of the Basel museum around Max Alioth were concerned with granting a second life to an existentially threatened building from the little-loved modern era by means of a change of usage. The Basel museum project was a plea for the continued existence of the built structure. In that respect it was way ahead of its time, so to speak, since now almost four decades ago it already voiced an architectural attitude which in recent years has become a key motif

tekturmuseums in Basel war ein Plädoyer für eine reale Kontinuität des Gebauten. Damit war es seiner Zeit weit voraus. Denn es formulierte schon vor knapp vier Jahrzehnten eine architektonische Haltung, die in den letzten Jahren zu einem zentralen Motiv der zeitgenössischen Architektur geworden ist und 2021 mit dem Pritzker-Preis an das französische Architektenpaar Anne Lacaton und Jean-Philippe Vassal auch weltweit gewürdigt wurde: Das Verständnis, dass Abriss von Architektur nicht die erste, sondern immer nur die letzte Option sein dürfe und Architekten immer versuchen sollten, die Lebensdauer des Bestehenden durch die empathische Adaption seiner Gestalt und Nutzung an die Bedürfnisse der Gegenwart zu verlängern.

Aber auch in museologischer Hinsicht beschritten die Gründer des Architekturmuseums neue Wege mit ihrer Entscheidung, das Museum vor allem für Wechselausstellungen und diskursive Veranstaltungen zu nutzen, aber auf den Aufbau einer Sammlung zu verzichten. Im damals (und weitestgehend auch noch heute) gängigen Museumsdiskurs galt die Sammlung als konstitutives Element eines Museums, um das kulturelle Erbe zu bewahren, zu erforschen und der Öffentlichkeit zu vermitteln. Das Bundesamt für Kultur betrachtet aufgrund dieses Fehlens einer Sammlung das Schweizerische Architekturmuseum für nicht qualifiziert, im Rahmen der Museumsförderung des Bundes eine Unterstützung zu erhalten. Manche sehen den Sammlungsverzicht deswegen als den Geburtsfehler der Gründung des Museums. Man könnte ihn aber auch als eine sehr bewusste Realisation der besonderen Disposition eines Architekturmuseums verstehen. Denn während in einem Kunstmuseum Kunstwerke ausgestellt werden so wie in einem Uhrenmuseum Uhren, kann ein Architekturmuseum nie die Werke der Architektur selbst ausstellen – also die Bauwerke –, sondern immer nur Darstellungen derselben in abstrahierter und verkleinerter Form. Deswegen steht das Publikum von Architekturmuseen immer vor der besonderen Herausforderung, sich das abwesende Bauwerk über den Umweg von Zeichnungen, Plänen,

of contemporary architecture, as borne out globally by the award of the Pritzker price 2021 to the French architecture couple Anne Lacaton and Jean-Philippe Vassal: namely, the belief that the demolition of architecture should never be the first but only ever the last option, and that architects should always attempt to extend the life of the existing by means of empathetically adapting its physical substance and use according to the needs of the present.

In museological respect, too, the founders of the Swiss Architecture Museum went new ways with their decision to primarily use the museum for temporary exhibitions and discursive events, but not to build up a permanent collection. According to the then prevalent museum discourse (and to a large extent still today), a collection was considered the constitutive feature of a museum for the purpose of preserving and researching cultural heritage and making it accessible to the general public. Due to its lack of a collection, the Federal Office of Culture does not consider the Swiss Architecture Museum sufficiently qualified to receive support under the federal government's museum subsidy programme. For that reason, some people regard the original decision to forego establishing a collection as a birth defect of the museum. However, once could also see it as the conscious realization of the special nature of an architectural museum. While an art museum has works of art to put on display and a watch museum shows watches, an architectural museum can, for good reasons, never show the works themselves – that is, the buildings – but only representations thereof on a smaller scale and in abstract form. This means that visitors always face the special challenge of having to imagine for themselves the absent building with the aid of sketches, plans, photographs, and models. The architecture itself is always beyond reach, never really actually present.

In his project for the German Architecture Museum, Oswald Mathias Ungers ingeniously brought this existential contradiction of any architectural museumto bear with his "house within a house": there you have an idealized house rising upwards through the struc-

Fotos und Modellen vorstellen zu müssen. Die Architektur selbst ist nie zum Greifen nah, nie wirklich da.

In seinem Projekt für das Deutsche Architekturmuseum hat Oswald Mathias Ungers diesen Daseinswiderspruch des Architekturmuseums auf geniale Weise mit seinem ‹Haus im Haus› zur Anschauung gebracht: Ein idealtypisches Haus zieht sich dort vertikal durch das Gebäude und kulminiert im obersten Geschoss mit einem abstrahierten Satteldach. Es ist der Platzhalter für die Architektur, die man im Architekturmuseum nicht unmittelbar ausstellen kann, gleichsam ein dreidimensionaler Trost des Publikums dafür, ihm die objektive Erfahrung von Architektur vorzuenthalten – und dies ausgerechnet in dem ihr gewidmeten Museum. In Basel haben Max Alioth und seine Mitstreiter dieses Dilemma noch direkter adressiert: Sie erklärten das Domus-Haus zum Architekturmuseum, so wie man eine Ausstellung für eröffnet erklärt. Sie taten das mit einer bis heute ansteckenden geistigen Unabhängigkeit und Chuzpe, die an Magrittes Umkehrdefinition der Wirklichkeit seines Gemäldes ‹Céci n'est pas une pipe› erinnert. Dass sie das Domus-Haus nicht nur als den Ort des Architekturmuseums verstanden wissen wollten, sondern tatsächlich auch als das normalerweise unmögliche Exponat im Massstab 1:1, verdeutlichte unmissverständlich die Eröffnungsausstellung des Museums im Jahr 1984. In ihrer legendären Rauminstallation ‹Wrapped Floors› verhüllten Christo und Jeanne-Claude vollständig die inneren Oberflächen des Gebäudes. Der Abbau der Ausstellung mag deswegen etwas von der Enthüllungsgeste gehabt haben, mit der von einem neu erworbenen Kunstwerk der Schleier gezogen wird, um es zum ersten Mal im Licht der Öffentlichkeit zu präsentieren.

Vielleicht ist das der Punkt, an dem wir Heutige das visionäre Gründungswerk von Max Alioth aufnehmen und weiterdenken sollten, auch und gerade in Bezug auf die Idee einer Architektursammlung. Denn wenn Alioth *et alii* das Domus-Haus als erstes Exponat des Architekturmuseums intendierten, könnten wir heute

ture, ending on the top floor with an abstracted gable roof. It serves as a placeholder for the architecture one can never exhibit one-to-one in a museum, a three-dimensional consolation, so to speak, for an audience that is deprived of experiencing architecture objectively – and this, of all things, in a museum of architecture. In Basel Max Alioth and his colleagues addressed this dilemma in an even more direct manner by declaring the Domus House an architecture museum just as one declares an exhibition open. They did this with chutzpah and an intellectual independence that reverberates to this day and which is reminiscent of René Magritte's reverse definition of reality in his famous painting *The Treachery of Reason* with its caption "Ceci n'est pas une pipe". The fact that they wanted the Domus House not only to be understood as the site of the architecture museum but also as its own – otherwise impossible – exhibit on a 1:1 scale was unmistakably borne out by the opening exhibition in 1984. In their legendary spatial installation *Wrapped Floors*, Christo and Jeanne-Claude completely veiled the surfaces within the building so that the dismantling of the exhibition had something of a gesture of disclosure to it, akin to the unveiling of a newly acquired work of art in its first presentation to the public.

Perhaps we have reached a point at which we today should revisit and think Max Alioth's visionary founding work a step further, not least with regard to the idea of architectural collections. Because if Alioth and his companions envisaged the Domus House as the Architecture Museum's first exhibit, we could now go one logical step further and designate it as the first item of a novel kind of architectural collection, which is not made up of representations of buildings but by the buildings themselves. The collection area would be identical with the territory of Switzerland, very much like in Jorge Luis Borges' short story *On Rigour in Science* in which cartographers create a map of their country on a 1:1 scale. A map that was not only congruent to scale with the territory it depicted but which, at the same time, had to make the latter disappear in order to be perceived itself. Like no other country in the world,

noch einen logischen Schritt weitergehen und es als erstes Stück einer neuartigen Architektursammlung begreifen, die nicht mehr aus Darstellungen von Gebäuden, sondern aus diesen Gebäuden selbst besteht. Das Sammlungsgebiet wäre identisch mit dem Territorium der Schweiz, analog zu Jorge Luis Borges' Kurzgeschichte ‹Von der Genauigkeit der Wissenschaft›, in der die Kartografen eines Landes eine Karte desselben im Massstab 1:1 erstellen. Eine Karte, die nicht nur massstäblich deckungsgleich mit dem von ihr dargestellten Territorium war, sondern es gleichzeitig zum Verschwinden bringen musste, um selbst betrachtet werden zu können. Die Schweiz wäre wie kein anderes Land der Welt prädestiniert für ein solches territoriales Architekturmuseum. Denn das Land im Herzen Europas bietet eine überdurchschnittliche Dichte qualitätvoller Architektur auf einem Territorium überschaubarer Grösse, das flächendeckend mit einem differenzierten öffentlichen Verkehr erschlossen ist. Es wäre möglich, die ganze Schweiz zum Schweizerischen Architekturmuseum zu erklären. Man bräuchte nur einen Katalog von Gebäuden zu bestimmen, anhand derer sich die Geschichte und Gegenwart der Schweizer Architektur gut erfahren liesse. Man sollte des Weiteren bei der Auswahl der Gebäude darauf achten, dass diese grundsätzlich öffentlich begehbar wären (zumindest zu bestimmten Zeiten). Und man müsste einen digitalen Sammlungskatalog in Form einer App oder Smartphone-fähigen Webseite erstellen, der alle Gebäude der Sammlung auflistet, bildliche und textliche Informationen enthält sowie die Standorte der Gebäude und ihre Besichtigungszeiten für das Publikum aufführt. Museum und Sammlung wären also räumlich nicht identisch. In den Räumen des Museums würden weiterhin Ausstellungen stattfinden, um mit Zeichnungen, Plänen, Modellen, Prototypen, Filmen, Fotografien, Computeranimationen, virtuellen Realitäten und dergleichen mehr die architektonische Neugier des Publikums zu erregen, Fragen aufzuwerfen, Gewissheiten zu erschüttern und Neuentdeckungen zu ermöglichen. Und wenn das Publikum am Ende der Ausstellung das Museum schliesslich ver-

Switzerland would be predestined to host such a territorial museum of architecture, given that the country in the heart of Europe has an above-average density of high-quality architecture to offer on a limited territory which is easily accessible by a sophisticated system of public transport. In my opinion it would by all means be possible to declare Switzerland as a whole as the Swiss Architecture Museum. All you would need is to establish a catalogue of buildings through which people could learn about the history of architecture in Switzerland and experience its present scope and quality. When choosing a selection of buildings, one should also ensure that they are accessible to the public (at least at certain times).

Furthermore, it would require a digital collection catalogue in the shape of an app or a smartphone-compatible website, which lists all the recorded buildings, contains information about them in the form of texts and images, and indicates the locations of the buildings and when they are open to the public. This means the museum and the collection would not be identical in spatial terms. In the museum's rooms one could continue to stage exhibitions to stimulate

Domus-Haus am Pfluggässlein 3 in Basel, 1984-2004 Sitz des Architekturmuseums

The Domus House at Pfluggässlein 3 in Basel, home of the Architecture Museum from 1984 to 2004

lässt, betritt es gleichsam eine zweite Ausstellung: die Wunderkammer unserer gebauten Wirklichkeit. Das wäre ein Architekturmuseum, wie es Max Alioth sicher auch gefallen würde.

the audience's architectural curiosity, raise questions, challenge certainties, and enable new discoveries with the aid of drawings, plans, models, prototypes, films, photographs, computer animations, virtual realities, etc. When visitors leave the museum after having taken in the exhibition, they step into a second exhibition, so to speak: the cabinet of curiosities of our built reality. That would be an architecture museum very much to the liking of Max Alioth.

Ausgewählte Bauten   Selected buildings

Haus am Rebberg

Unterer Rebbergweg 124, Reinach, 1961

35 Wohnhaus des Architekten, Ansicht von Westen — The architect's home, view from the west

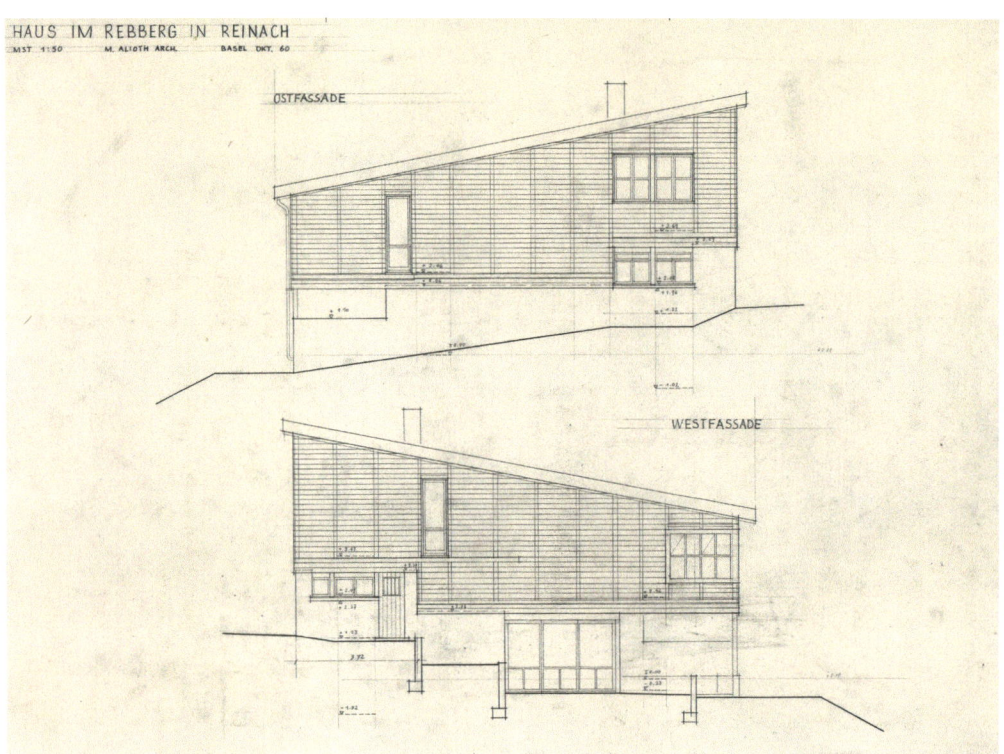

Ost- und Westfassade — Façades towards the east and west

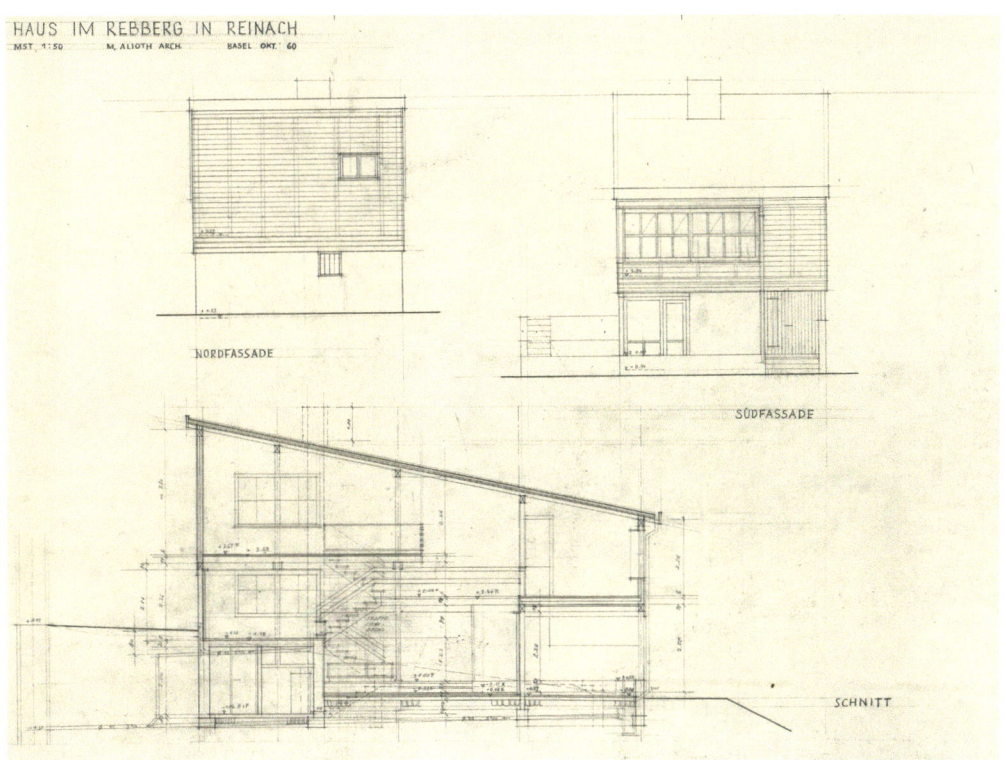

Nord- und Südfassade und Schnitt
Grundrisse Keller, Erdgeschoss und Galerie, S. 38–39

Façades towards the north and the south, and cross-section
Floorplans cellar, ground floor, and gallery, pp. 38–39

HAUS IM REBBERG IN REINACH
MST. 1:50   M. ALIOTH ARCH.   BASEL OKT. 60

KELLER

ERDGESCHOSS

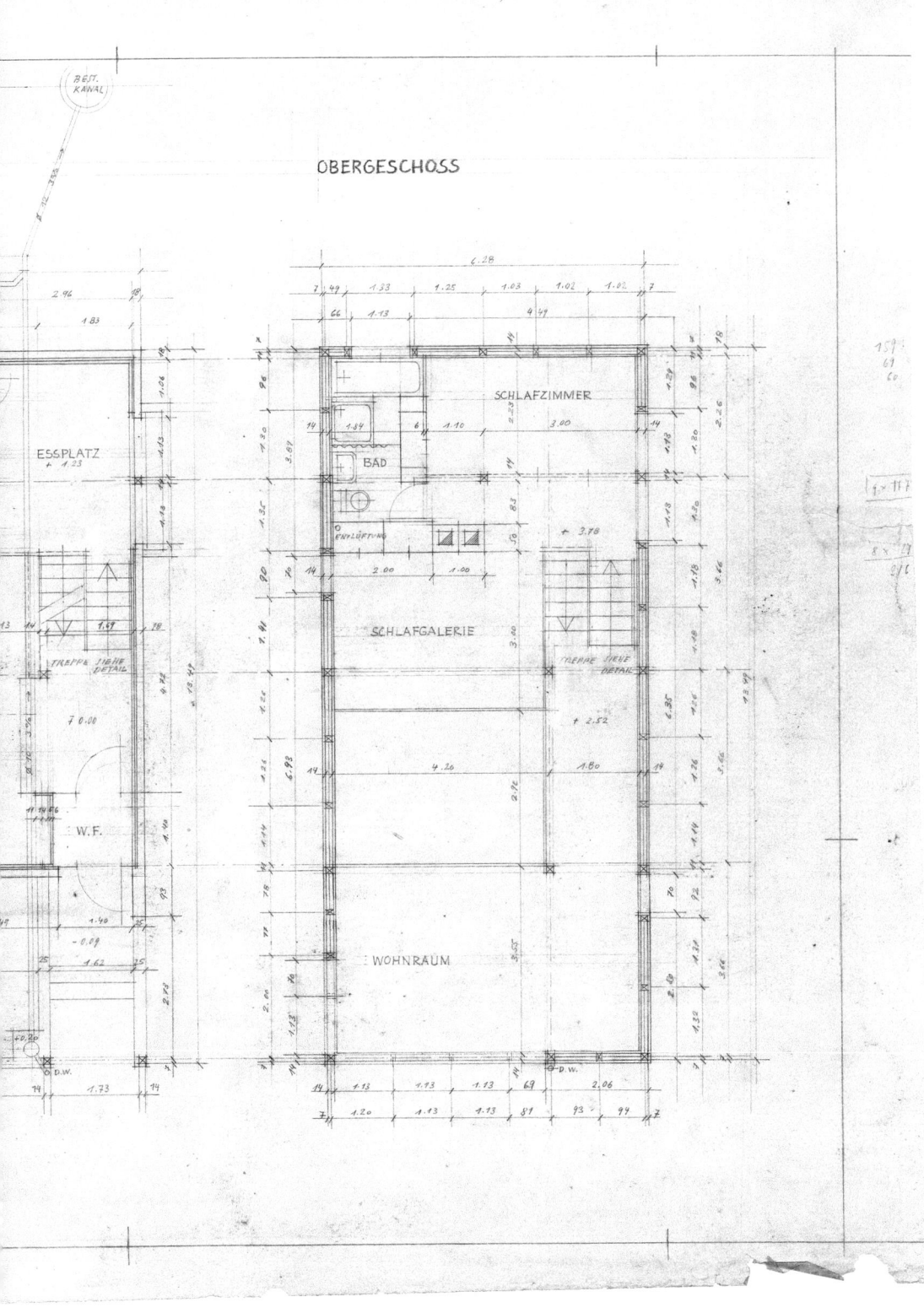

Das ‹erste Haus des Architekten›: Max Alioth konnte sein erstes Haus für sich selber bauen, an bevorzugter Südlage am Reinacher Rebberg. Die Form des Grundstücks erlaubte ein Haus von nur gerade 6 m Breite. Im Innern öffnet sich eine Wohnhalle über eineinhalb Geschosse und ermöglichte – in Entsprechung zur Hanglage – die Einführung von versetzten Geschossen und einer Galerie.

Betonsockel, Holzständerkonstruktion, Backsteinmauerwerk und Eternitschindelverkleidung vermitteln eine Architekturauffassung der Unmittelbarkeit und der Genügsamkeit, wie sie in der Tradition des Neuen Bauens (in Basel Paul Artaria und Ernst Egeler) auch in der Nachkriegszeit unter dem Einfluss skandinavischer oder US-amerikanischer Architektur vorbildlich blieb.

Treppe aus dem Erdgeschoss auf die Galerie — Staircase leading from the ground floor to the gallery

The "architect's first house": the first house Max Alioth designed and constructed was actually his own home situated on a sunny, south-facing slope in the vineyards of Reinach. The shape of the plot allowed for a house not measuring more than six metres in width. Inside, the living hall opens up over one and a half floors and – in correspondence with the sloping site – facilitated the installation of offset floors and an open gallery.

The concrete foundation, a post and beam construction, brick masonry, and the Eternit cladding panels convey an architectural conception of immediacy and frugality in line with the tradition of modernist architecture (in Basel Paul Artaria and Ernst Egeler) and enhanced by the influence of Scandinavian and US-American architecture in the post-war period.

Altershotel Dalbehof

Kapellenstrasse 17, Basel, 1972–1974 und 1983/1984

Blick in den Park zwischen den Wohnhäusern · View of the park between the apartment blocks

Auf dem parkähnlichen Grundstück einer ehemaligen Villa gruppierten die Architekten Alioth und Remund die Altersresidenz mit 42 Wohnungen als aufgelockerte Anlage zwischen alten Bäumen. Die mit allem Komfort ausgestattete Einrichtung richtet sich an ältere Menschen mit gehobenen Ansprüchen. Das verbindende Sockelgeschoss umfasst die Gemeinschaftseinrichtungen, während die Wohnungen zu zwei und drei Zimmern in zwei punktförmig organisierten hohen Häusern untergebracht sind – mit allseitig schöner Aussicht auf den Park. Das Angebot von selbstständigen Wohnungen wird ergänzt durch Service-Leistungen, darunter ein Speisesaal, Aufenthaltsräume, Gästezimmer, Therapieräume, Krankenstation und ein Hallenbad. In der zweiten Etappe korrigierten die Architekten das Programm zugunsten etwas grösserer Wohnungen mit eigener Küche.

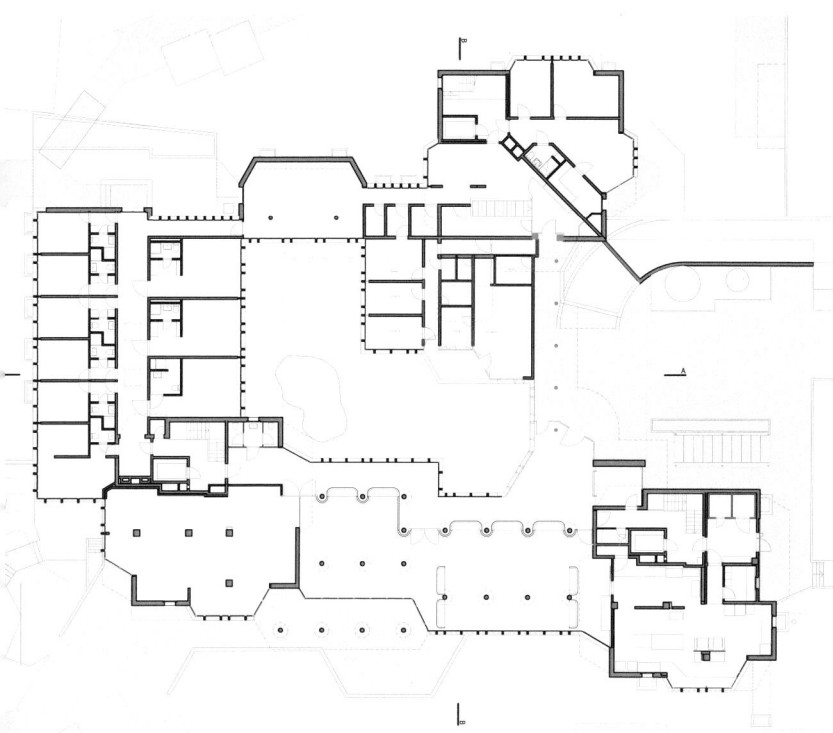

On the park-like grounds of a former villa, Alioth and Remund designed a senior citizen residence consisting of 42 apartments as a dispersed complex between the old trees. The facility equipped with all amenities was aimed at elderly people with sophisticated tastes. The connecting basement contained all the required communal facilities, while the two- and three-bedroom apartments were housed in two punctiform high-rise buildings with a view on to the park on all sides. The advantage of independent living was complemented by a range of services including a common dining hall, lounges, guest rooms, therapy facilities, a sick bay, and an indoor swimming pool. In a second phase, the architects realigned the programme in favour of somewhat larger apartments with an in-built kitchen.

Gartenhöfe im Innern der Anlage und Parkpartien zwischen den hohen Wohnhäusern

Garden courtyard within the complex, and park areas between the apartment blocks

Speisesaal und Schwimmhalle　　　　Dining room and indoor swimming pool

Mehrfamilienhaus

Pfeffingerstrasse 48/50, Basel, 1976

55 Abgeschrägte Balkon- und Erkerräume — Angled balcony and bay spaces

Die Erker auf der Strassen- und die Balkone auf der Gartenseite sorgen für eine willkommene Ausweitung des Wohnraums

The bays facing the street and the balconies towards the garden create a welcome extension to the living space

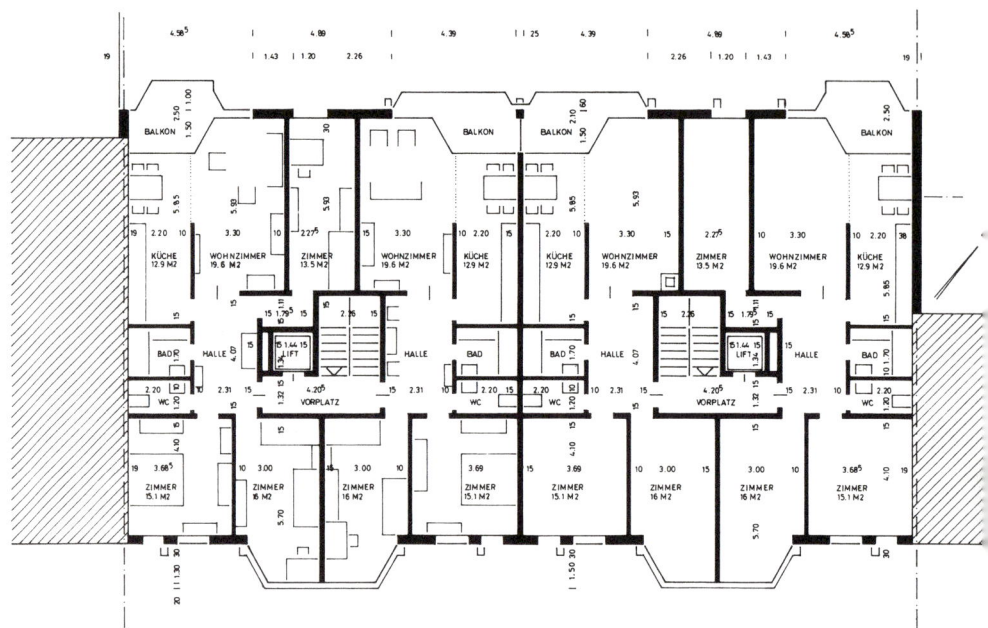

Die Mehrfamilienhäuser aus der Gründerzeit wurden von der Bauherrschaft, einer Pensionskasse, durch neue, im Gundeldingerquartier typologisch verankerte Wohnhäuser ersetzt. Die kleinteilige Gliederung der Fassaden schafft eine massstäbliche Verbindung zu den Nachbarhäusern. Der Mauerverband, die farblich abgesetzten Gurtgesimse und die differenziert ausgestalteten Balkonbrüstungen sind ungewöhnlich sorgfältig durchgearbeitet und mit Blick auf die Massverhältnisse der Umgebung austariert. Die Gartengestaltung erleichtert den Gebrauch durch die Mieterschaft.

Grundriss des Regelgeschosses   Ground plan of standard upper floor

The original, 19th-century apartment buildings were replaced on the developers' orders – a pension fund – by a set of new multi-family houses that typologically fitted the style of the Gundeldinger District. The small-scale structure of the façades is aligned with the appearance of the neighbouring houses. The masonry bond, the cornices in contrasting colours, and the elaborately designed balcony parapets are unusually carefully designed and in balance with the dimensional ratio of the surrounding environment. The garden layout facilitates use on the part of the tenants.

The architects placed particular emphasis on the appealingly designed passage leading from the lowered ground floor to the garden, pp. 60–61

Antikenmuseum Basel und Sammlung Ludwig

St. Alban-Graben 5 und 7, Basel, 1986–1988

Blick in den infolge des Umbaus und der Erweiterung im Untergeschoss neu gewonnenen Ausstellungsraum

View of the new exhibition space created by the extension and refurbishment of the basement

Die beiden klassizistischen Wohnhäuser von Melchior Berri (1826, resp. 1826–1828) dienten unterschiedlichen Zwecken, bis 1964–1966 im Haus Nr. 5 das neu geschaffene Antikenmuseum eingerichtet wurde. Den rückwärtigen Oberlichtsaal am Luftgässlein schuf Kantonsbaumeister Hans Luder. Seit 1979 studierten Stadt und Museum Erweiterungsvarianten, darunter auch einen Erweiterungsbau anstelle der Pfandleihanstalt am Luftgässlein. In einem Studienauftrag hatten Alioth und Remund einen Neubau vorgeschlagen. In der politischen Diskussion obsiegte dann allerdings das Modell ‹Rochade›, wonach das zweite Berri-Haus, Nr. 7, in den Museumskomplex eingebunden wurde (und das Zivilstandsamt an die Rittergasse umzog).

Durch den neu geschaffenen Verbindungstrakt gelang es, die Gäste auf einen abwechslungsreichen Rundgang durch das Museum zu leiten. Die beiden Stadtvillen ebenso wie der Oberlichtsaal aus den 1960er Jahren erwiesen sich durch die sorgsamen Ergänzungen ein weiteres Mal als idealer Rahmen für die Ausstellung von Werken der Antike.

Umbau der beiden klassizistischen Villen von Melchior Berri (1826–1828) zum erweiterten Museum (1986–1988). Im Hintergrund die erste Erweiterung des Oberlichtsaals von Hans Luder (1964–1966)

Conversion of the two classicist villas by Melchior Berri (1826–1828) to create the extended museum. In the background the first extension of the skylight room designed by Hans Luder (1964–1966)

The two neo-classical residential buildings built by Melchior Berri (1826 and 1826–1828, respectively) served different purposes until, in 1964–1966, house No. 5 was chosen as the venue for the newly established Antikenmuseum. The skylight room at the rear facing the Luftgässlein was designed by cantonal architect Hans Luder. Since 1979, the museum and city authorities had been discussing possible ways of extending the museum, including the option of a new wing in place of the pawn office on the Luftgässlein. In a commissioned study, Alioth and Remund had proposed a new museum building but, in the end, the model "Rochade" came out top in the political debate, according to which the second Berri house, No. 7, was to be integrated into the museum complex (and the civil registry office instead moved to Rittergasse).

The new connecting wing allowed visitors to be channelled through the museum space on a highly varied tour. In the end, the two town mansions along with the skylight room from the 1960s, and thanks to a few thoughtful additions, proved to be the ideal setting for the exhibition of works of antiquity.

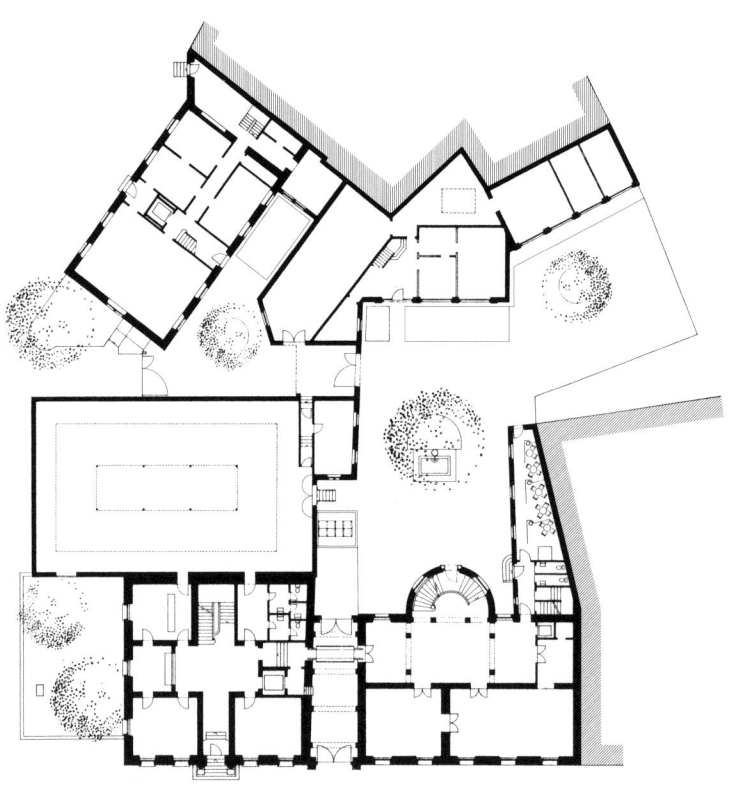

Grundriss des Erdgeschosses — Ground floor layout

Blick aus dem Obergeschoss des grösseren Hauses (Haus Nr. 7) ins Vestibül

View from the upper floor of the larger house (House No. 7) into the lobby

Verbindungsbrücke zwischen den beiden neu zusammengefassten ehemaligen Wohnhäusern

Connecting bridge between the two newly joined, former residential buildings

Haus für zwei

Oberlichter in den beiden oberen Geschossen — Skylights on the two upper floors

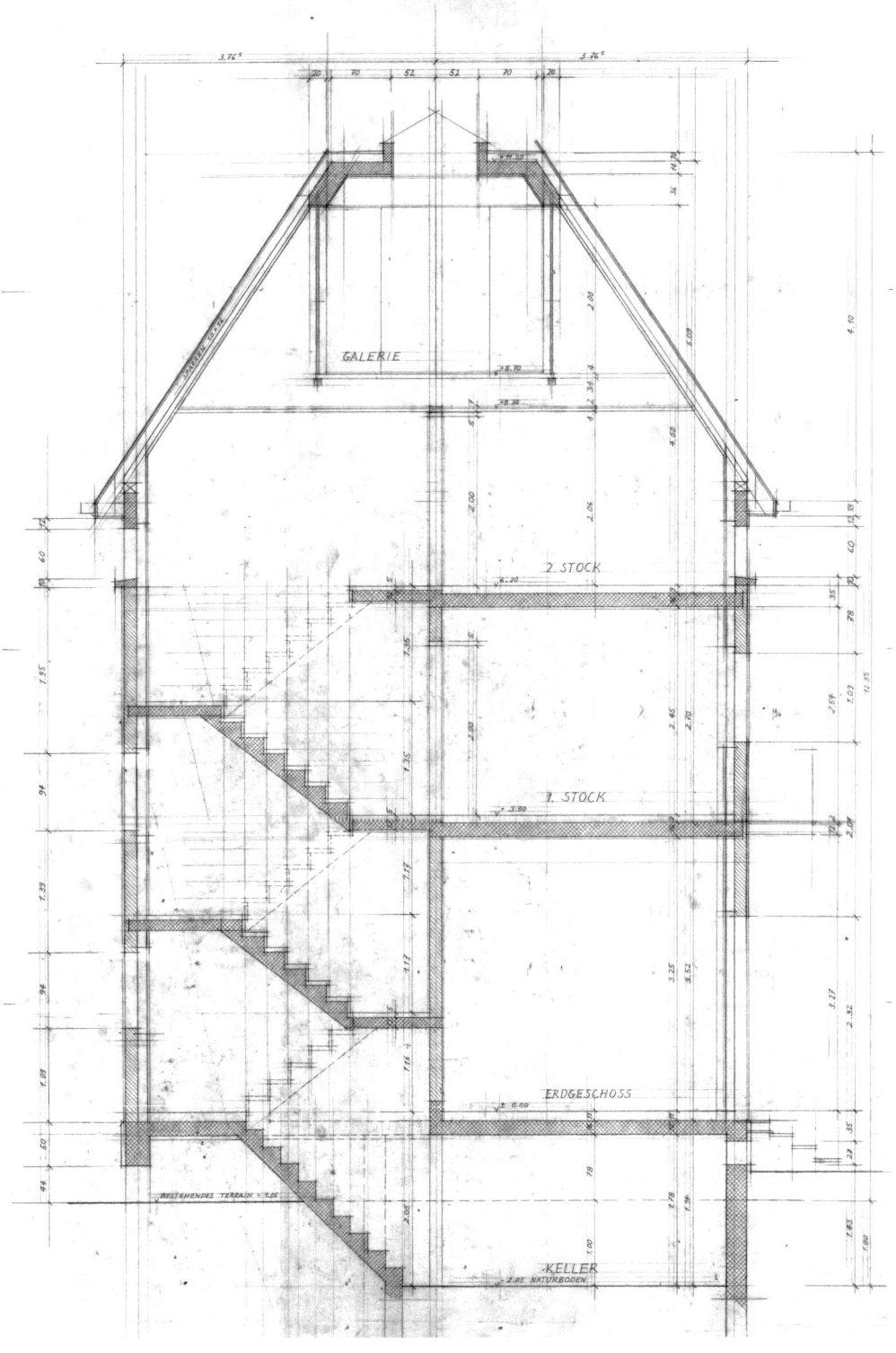

Querschnitt durch das Treppenhaus — Cross-section of the stairwell

Ansicht von der Strassenseite — View from the street

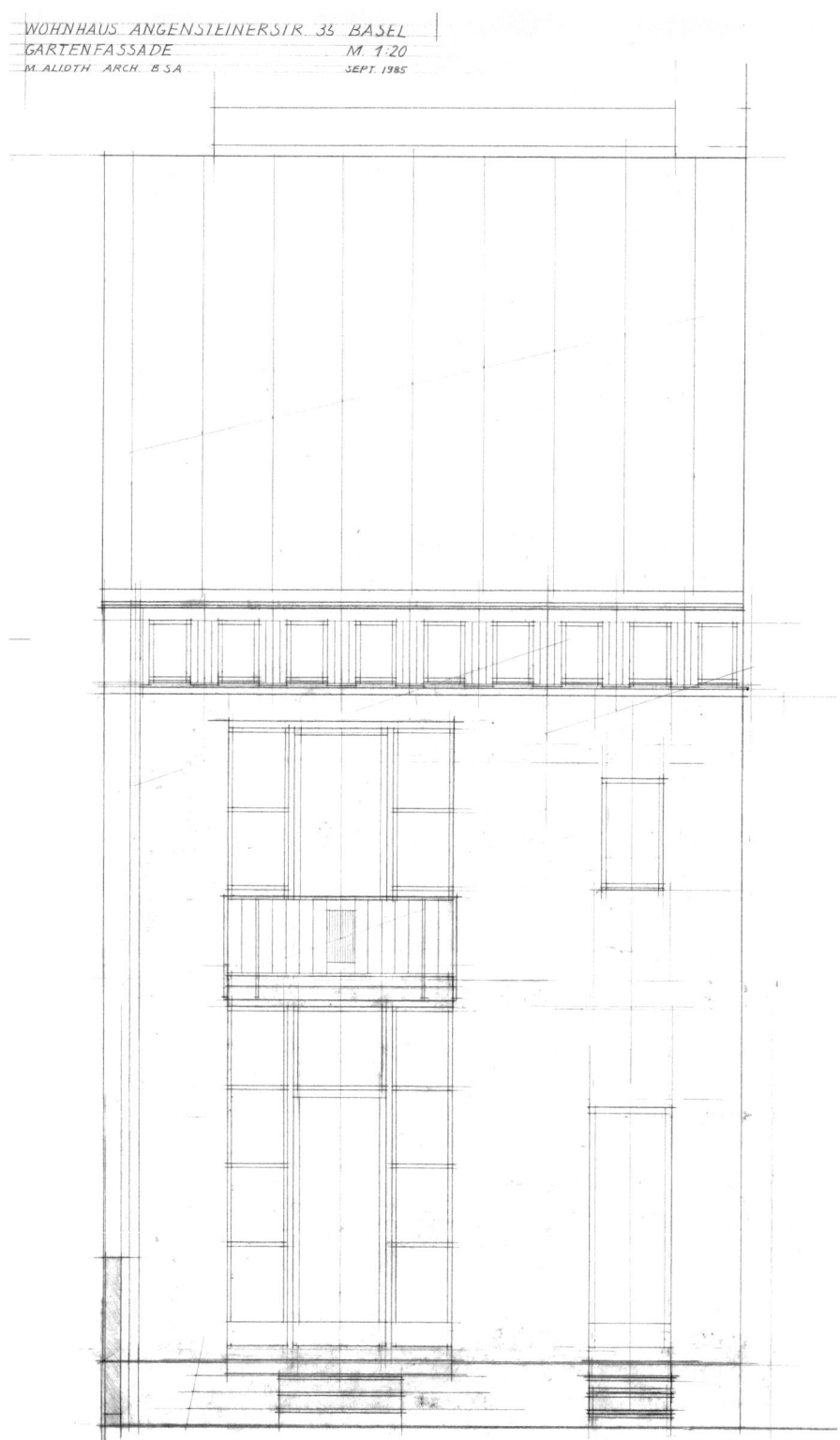

Ansicht von der Gartenseite — View from the garden

Auf einem knappen Restgrundstück von 90 m² baute Alioth in bevorzugter Lage für seine Frau und sich auf nur rund 45 m² ein viergeschossiges Haus. Zu beachten waren die Schutzzone in dieser noch immer einheitlich bebauten Quartierstrasse im Gellert und eine schützenswerte Blutbuche im Vorgarten. Das überhohe Erdgeschoss mit Esszimmer und Küche öffnet sich auf den kleinen Gartenhof. Darüber folgt das Schlafgeschoss mit Bibliothek und weiter oben der Wohn- und Arbeitsraum, der sich über zwei Geschosse in den Dachraum mit Galerie ausdehnt.

    Die Auseinandersetzung mit den historischen Nachbarbauten führte zu architektonischen Entscheidungen, die – in den 1980er Jahren – eine Relativierung der Formideale der klassischen Moderne einschlossen: Symmetrie und Asymmetrie und steile Quergiebel in der Fassadenbildung, eine dekorativ einbezogene Brandmauer in Bruchstein, hochrechteckige, tief eingeschnittene Fenster und eine raffinierte Lichtregie.

On a small, left-over plot of 90 sqm. in a choice neighbourhood, Alioth built a four-storey house for his wife and himself, measuring not more than 45 sqm. The only things he had to consider on this still homogenously built, quiet street in the posh Gellert neighbourhood were the protection zone and a valuable, old copper beech in the front garden. The raised ground-floor accommodating the dining room and kitchen looked out on to a small patio garden. Above that was a bedroom with a library, and yet further up a living room and a study that stretched across two floors into a gallery under the roof.

    Alignment with the historical houses next-door prompted him to make architectural decisions, which – in the 1980s – implied a relativization of the formal ideals of classic modernism: symmetry and asymmetry and steep transverse gables on the façade, a decoratively incorporated, ashlar firewall, high rectangular, deeply recessed windows, and a refined lighting control.

View over the back garden wall

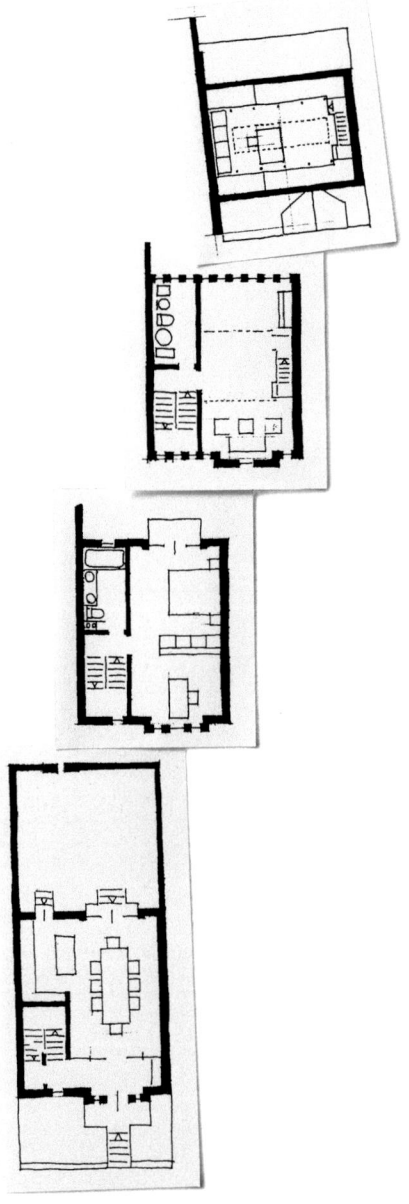

Grundrisse über vier Geschosse　　　Ground plans of the four floors

81 Treppenhaus entlang der bestehenden Brandmauer   Stairwell following the existing firewall

Küche und Essraum mit Blick in den Garten · Kitchen and dining room with a view of the garden

Zweigeschossiger Wohnraum im zweiten Obergeschoss
Schlafzimmer im ersten Obergeschoss

Two-storey living space on the second floor
Bedroom on the first floor

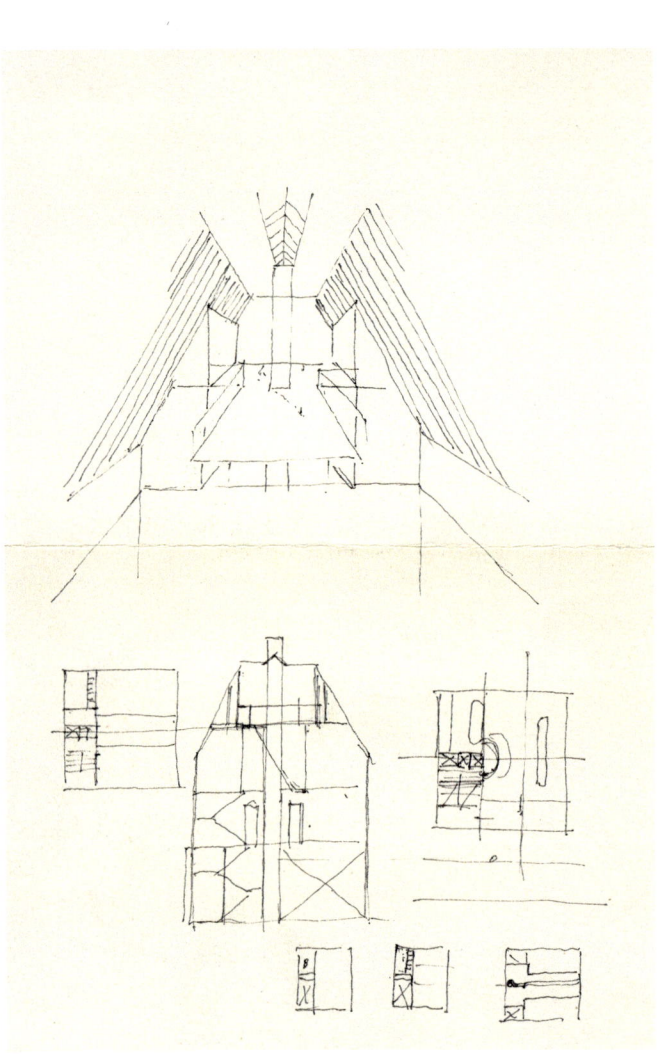

École Supérieure des Arts Visuels (ÉSAV)

Marrakesch-Amerchich, Marokko, 2005–2007

Eingangsbereich mit Kakteengarten — Entrance area with cactus garden

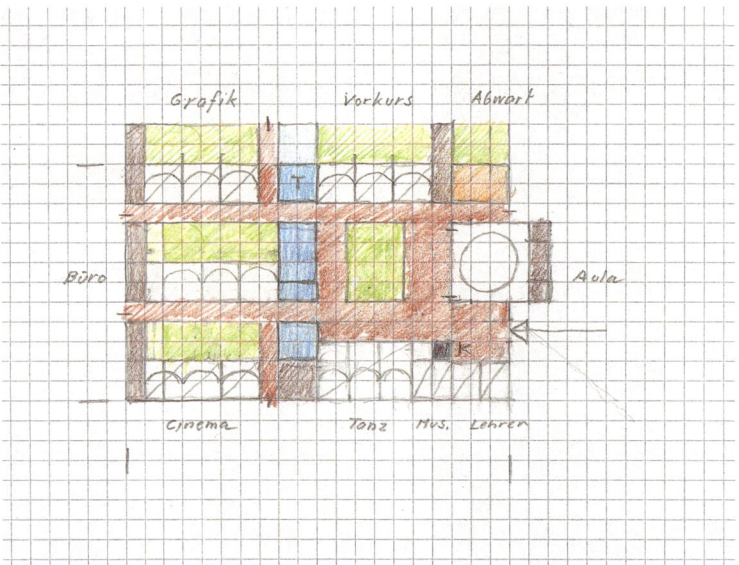

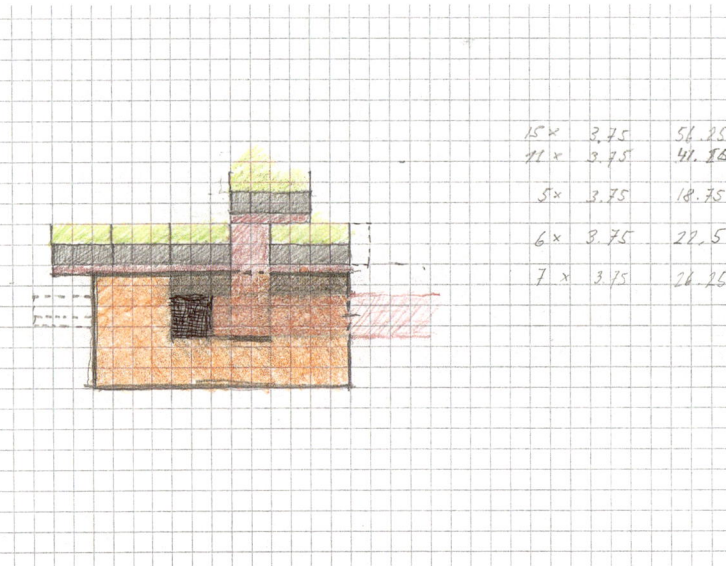

Variantenstudium — Study of variants

Studienmodell — Study model

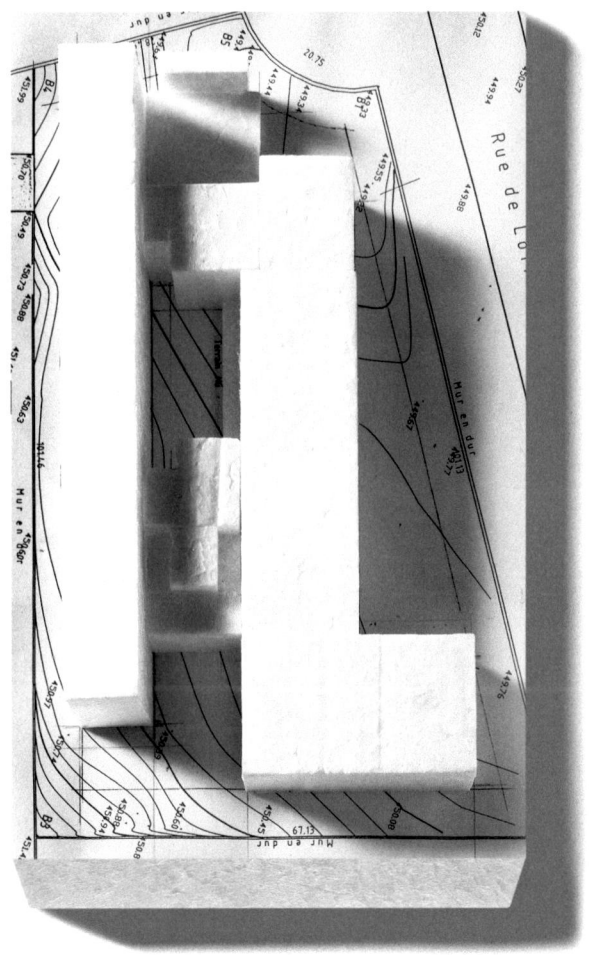

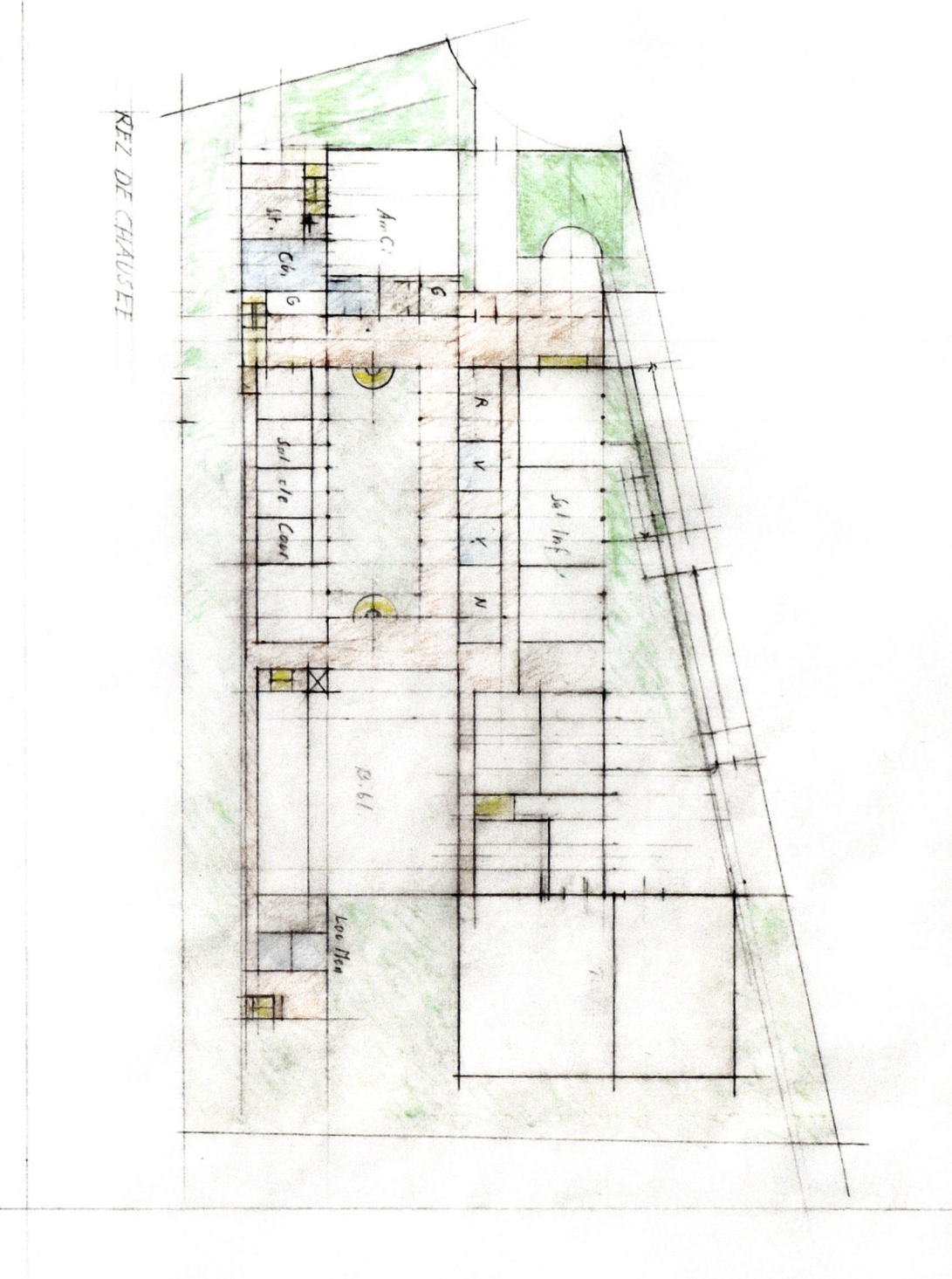

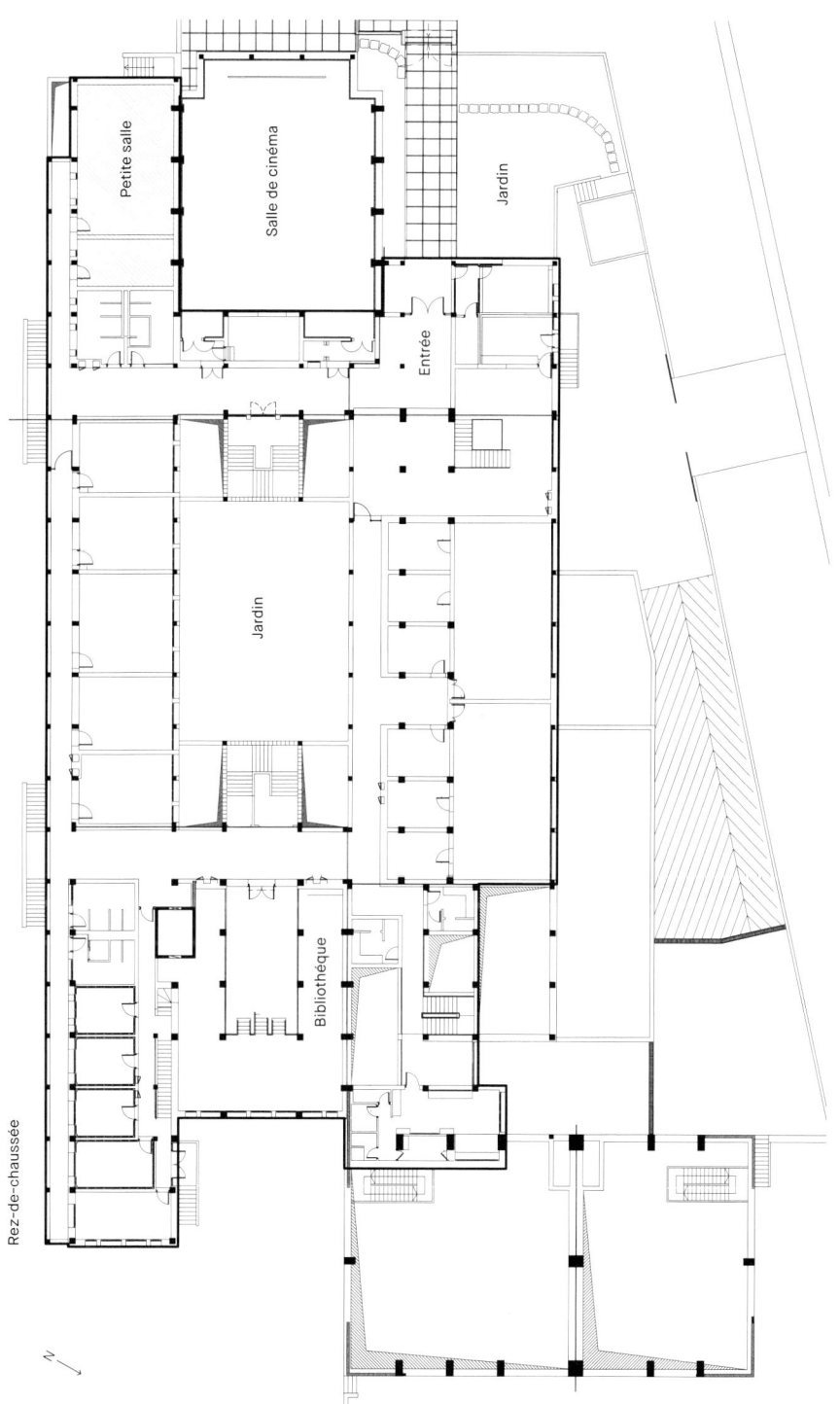

97 Grundriss Erdgeschoss   Floor plan of ground floor

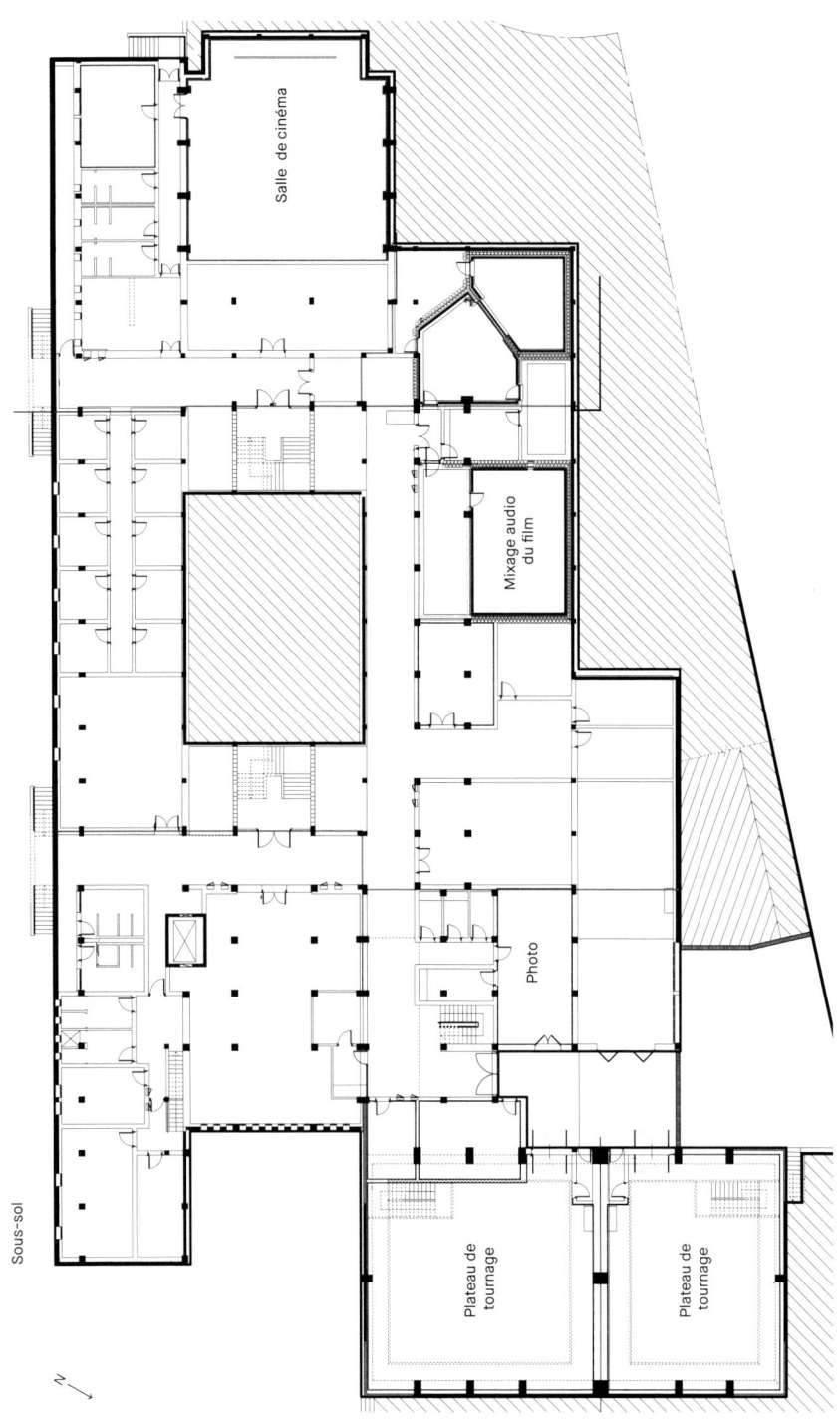

Grundriss Untergeschoss · Floor plan of basement

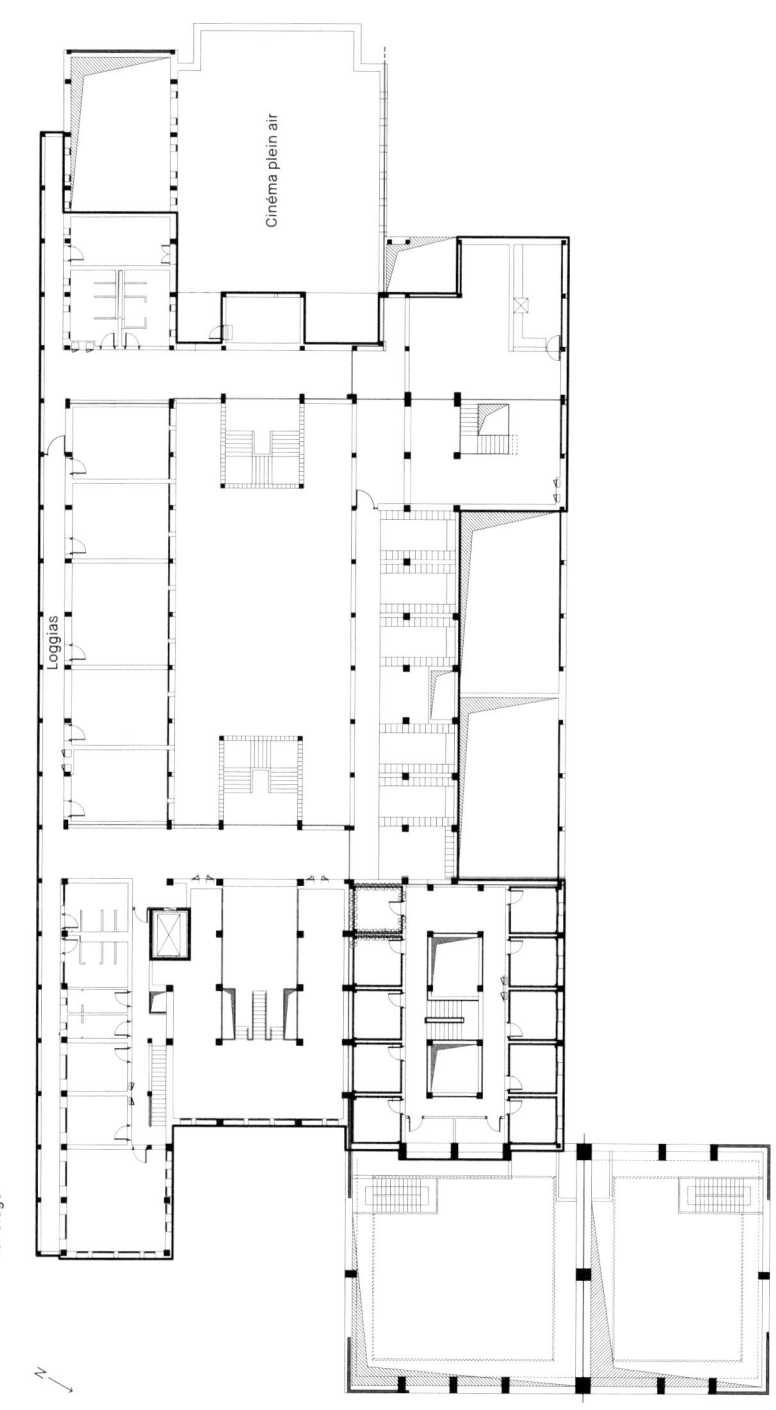

99 Grundriss 1. Obergeschoss   Floor plan of 1st floor

Mit dem Anliegen, die Pflege der marokkanischen Kultur auch in der gestalterischen Ausbildung von jungen Menschen aus dem Lande selber zu verankern, verbanden Max Alioth und Susanna Biedermann (1943–2007) die Gründung des Kulturhauses Dar Bellarj und der Hochschule für visuelle Kunst in Partnerschaft mit der Cadi Ayyad-Universität. Max Alioth: «Selbstverständliches zu tun ist heute eine Ausnahme. Im Grunde ist es einfach: nicht Geld schicken, sondern direkt vor Ort etwas bewirken».

Im Herzen der Medina von Marrakesch fanden sie für das Kulturzentrum ein Haus mit prächtigen Stuck- und Holzdekorationen, das sie originalgetreu restaurierten. Seid 1999 finden darin vielfältige Aktivitäten statt: Ausstellungen, Konzerte, Erzählstunden, Gesang, Tanz, Lesungen, Theateraufführungen und Workshops für Kinder und Erwachsene (siehe Seite 168).

Max Alioth und Susanna Biedermann waren überzeugt, dass Künstler:innen für die menschliche Entwicklung von Gesellschaften eine zentrale Rolle spielen. ‹Sehen lernen› war das Ziel, das sie sich für junge Menschen aus Afrika mit dem Bau der Hochschule für visuelle Kunst ÉSAV in Marrakesch setzten. In Partnerschaft mit der Cadi Ayyad-Universität konnten sie auf deren Grundstück

When Max Alioth and Susanna Biedermann (1943–2007) founded the cultural centre Dar Bellarj and the School of Visual Arts in cooperation with the Cadi Ayyad University, they did it with the aim of including design education for young Moroccan men and women as part of a plan to preserve Moroccan culture. Max Alioth: "Doing the obvious has become the exception these days. Basically, it's quite easy: don't merely send money, instead, try to bring about change on site."

At the centre of Marrakech's medina, they found an old house decorated in beautiful stucco and wood which they refurbished true to the original design. Since 1999 it has served as a venue for a wide range of activities: exhibitions, concerts, storytelling, song, dance, reading sessions, theatre performances, along with workshops for adults and children (see page 168).

Max Alioth and Susanna Biedermann were convinced that artists had a key role to play in moving society on in way that benefitted all its members. "Learning to see" was their envisioned goal for young African men and women when setting up the School of Visual Arts in Marrakech. In partnership with the Cadi Ayyad University they were able to make their generous engagement come true on the grounds of the university itself. Work began in 2003 in collaboration with the future director of the school, Vincent Melilli, and the designer Yves Dessuant, who developed the overall architectural programme. Max Alioth was responsible for the planning, devised the building concept and the ground plan, which the architect Khalil Benanni then went on to implement and further develop according to Max Alioth's ideas. Susanna Biedermann, Stéphanie Plassier, and Nathalie Locatelli created the interior design.

The openness of the school with its ever-changing ideas and surprising scenarios certainly had an influence on the design of the building. At the same time, the open construction allows the air to circulate during the hot summer season. The building's exterior is modelled on the city's ochre-red appearance. Vincent Melilli compared the 9,000 sqm. building with a seashell: dark on

ihr grosszügiges Engagement verwirklichen. Ab 2003 begannen die Arbeiten mit dem zukünftigen Direktor der Schule, Vincent Melilli, und dem Designer Yves Dessuant, der das architektonische Programm erstellte. Max Alioth initiierte die Planung, entwarf das Gebäudekonzept und die Grundrisse des Projekts, das der Architekt Khalil Bennani gemäss der Vision von Max Alioth respektvoll umsetzte und weiterentwickelte. Susanna Biedermann, Stéphane Plassier und Nathalie Locatelli schufen die Innenarchitektur.

Die Offenheit der Schule, wo wechselnde Ideen und überraschende Szenarien möglich werden, hat den Entwurf des Gebäudes beeinflusst. Das offene Gebäude lässt aber auch die Luft zirkulieren während der heissen Jahreszeit. Die ockerrote Stadt gibt dem Äusseren die Farbe. Das 9000 m² grosse Gebäude wird von Vincent Melilli mit einer Muschel verglichen: aussen dunkel und innen weiss. Das indirekte Licht und die weisse Farbe im Innern bilden ideale Voraussetzungen für die Schulräume. Die Gestaltung der Südfassade wirkt wie ein Vorhang vor den Loggien, in dessen Schatten sich die Luft abkühlt. Im Atrium erinnert die Anordnung der Öffnungen an den beiden Treppentürmen, die von marokkanischer Architektur inspiriert sind, auch an die Perforationslöcher von alten Zelluloid-Filmrollen. Seit 2007 lernen die Studierenden Geschichten zu erzählen, Bild- und Klangwelten zu erfinden, Filme, audiovisuelle Medien, Grafik und Digitaldesign zu produzieren. Sie fühlen sich in der Schule so wohl, dass sie nicht mehr weg wollen.

the outside, white inside. The indirect light and the white interior create ideal conditions in the classrooms. The southern façade is designed like a curtain fronting the loggias, allowing the air to cool in its shade. In the central courtyard, the apertures on the two stairwell towers, inspired by traditional Moroccan architecture, are reminiscent of the sprocket holes on old celluloid films. Since 2007, students have been learning how to tell stories, create worlds of sound and images, and produce films, audiovisual media, graphics, and digital design. They feel so at home there that they never want to leave.

Südfassade mit Laubengang und ‹brise-soleil› Southern façade with arcade and "brise-soleil"

Durchbrochene Wand im Treppenhaus mit Blick in den inneren Hof, S. 108–109

Openwork wall in the stairwell with view of inner courtyard, pp. 108–109

Die Anordnung der Öffnungen an den beiden Treppentürmen erinnert an die Perforationslöcher von alten Zelluloid-Filmrollen

The positioning of the apertures on the two stairwell towers is reminiscent of the sprocket holes on old celluloid films

Filmset und Kino   Film set and cinema   114

115 Offene Dachterrasse mit Freilichtkino, S. 116–117   Roof-top terrace with open air cinema, pp. 116–117

Blick auf Marrakesch und das Atlasgebirge — View towards Marrakech and Atlas Mountains

Die Kunsthochschule von Max Alioth und Susanna Biedermann in Marrakesch

Vincent Melilli

Max war nicht sehr gesprächig. An seiner Seite habe ich gelernt, zu schweigen und zu schauen. Er arbeitete an den Plänen für die Schule, der École Supérieure des Arts Visuels in Marrakesch (ÉSAV), die wir zusammen bauen und die wir mit seiner Frau Susanna Biedermann auch leiten sollten, sie die Abteilung ‹graphisme› und ich diejenige des ‹cinéma›. Kein Computer, Max zeichnete. Auf grosse karierte Blätter zog er Linien.

Ich fragte ihn, was er hier tue. Das Programm der Schule, geschweige denn das Raumprogramm standen noch nicht fest. Vielleicht müsse er wieder von vorne beginnen. Ich weiss, antwortete Max, das ist nicht schlimm, ich definiere die Volumen, und danach geht alles ganz rasch.

Und in der Tat. Kaum war das Programm gegeben, zeichnete Max die Pläne für die Schule, wie sie heute dasteht, in nicht einmal vierzehn Tagen.

Ich entsinne mich eines Gesprächs, im Laufe dessen ich bemerkte, dass Film projiziertes Licht sei und dass es ein Vorteil sein könnte, wenn das Gebäude selbst ein Lichtfänger wäre. Ich erhielt keine Antwort, kein Zeichen der Zustimmung. Wenn ich heute durch die Schule gehe, denke ich oft an dieses Gespräch – erst recht, wenn ich die Treppe hinuntersteige, was ich oft nur tue, um das Vergnügen des wechselnden Lichteinfalls zu geniessen.

Mehr noch als ein Lichtfänger zu sein, bieten die Öffnungen im Treppenhaus gerahmte Ausschnitte und Durchblicke. Die Öffnungen halten die Bewegungen fest. Man erblickt Menschen, die am Ausschnitt einer Öffnung vorbeigehen, und der Betrachter ergänzt die Bewegung im Raum beim Auftauchen des ‹Darstellers› in einer nächsten Öffnung. Die horizontalen Verschiebungen, wenn man sich auf einem Geschoss bewegt, und die vertikalen Bewegungen,

Max Alioth and Susanna Biedermann's School of Visual Arts in Marrakech

Vincent Melilli

Max was not the talkative type. At his side I learned to keep quiet and to observe. He worked on the plans for the school, the École Supérieure des Arts Visuels in Marrakech (ÉSAV) that we built together, and which we and his wife, Susanna Biedermann, would go on to manage, she in her capacity as head of "graphic art", I as head of "cinema". No computer, Max drew – he drew lines on large sheets of squared paper.

I asked him what he was doing. The curriculum had not yet been finalized, let alone the design of the rooms in the building. He might end up having to start from scratch. I know, Max replied; that wouldn't be so bad. He said he was defining its volumes; things move quickly once that's done.

And indeed they did: hardly had the curriculum been set, Max produced the design for the school as it stands today in just under two weeks.

I recall a discussion during which I commented that film is projected light and that it might be of advantage if the building itself were able to catch the light. He didn't reply; he showed no signs of agreement. When I walk around the school today, I often think back to that discussion – all the more when I take the stairs, which is something I often do just to enjoy the play of light within the stairwell.

More than being able to catch the light, the openings in the stairwell frame sequences and views. Its openings capture movement. One glimpses people walking past an opening; and when the "actor" appears in the next opening, the viewer fills in the unseen movements. When walking along a corridor, viewers make their own horizontal film; when going up or down the stairs to another floor, their film is a vertical one.

wenn man die Etagen wechselt – man macht sich beim Gang durch die Schule seinen eigenen Film.

Auch mit den klimatischen Verhältnissen hat sich Max intensiv beschäftigt. Es ist heiss in Marrakesch, doch erhebt sich unweit südlich der Stadt der Hohe Atlas, und im Winter, wenn Schnee die Gipfel bedeckt, fallen die Temperaturen und können auch die Null-Grad-Grenze erreichen. Wie lassen sich diese starken Temperaturunterschiede meistern und dabei der Energieverbrauch gering halten? Die Ausrichtung des Gebäudes macht sich die kühlen Luftströmungen zunutze. Die Südfassade ist als ‹brise soleil› ausgebildet: Die über eine Länge von mehr als 200 m verlaufenden horizontalen Betonblenden lassen die Luft zirkulieren und halten die Sonneneinstrahlung ab. Die Aussenwand ist als Backsteinmauerwerk in zwei Schalen mit einem Zwischenraum ausgeführt. Die 12-Loch-Backsteine wurden eigens für die Schule gebrannt. Von Norden fällt dagegen Licht durch grosse Fenster in die Ateliers der Bildhauer und der Grafikerinnen. Dank dieser Disposition wird es nie heiss in der Schule, auch nicht bei 45 °C Aussentemperatur. Um im Winter die Kälte in den Griff zu bekommen, hat Max mit Experten aus der Schweiz zusammengearbeitet, die den Einsatz von ‹puits canadiens› (kanadische Brunnen) vorgeschlagen haben, um die grossen Innenräume (Bibliothek, Kinosaal und grosser Unterrichtsraum) zu beheizen und zu kühlen. Dabei wird frische Luft von aussen durch im Boden verlegte Rohre angesogen und durch die träge Erdwärme temperiert in den Innenraum gebracht.

In der Architektur des Schulgebäudes verarbeitete Max Anregungen aus dem traditionellen marokkanischen Bauen ebenso wie solche der maghrebinischen Moderne. Der zentrale Innenhof entspricht dem von oben belichteten Riad in den innenstädtischen Hofhäusern. Andere Motive kennt man etwa von Guéliz, dem ersten, unter französischer Herrschaft ab 1913 erbauten Quartier der ‹ville nouvelle› von Marrakesch. Und den ‹brise soleil› kennt man von europäisch geprägten Bauten der 1950er Jahre. Dieser Ansatz ist seit dem Bau der ÉSAV vorbildlich für die jüngere Architektur in Marrakesch.

Max also closely addressed the climatic conditions. It is hot in Marrakech, but the High Atlas mountain range rises not far south of the city, and in the winter, when its peaks are covered in snow, temperatures in the city fall and can reach freezing level. How does one deal with such temperature extremes, and keep energy consumption low? The building's alignment makes use of cooling air currents, with its south-facing façade designed as a brise-soleil: over 200 m, its concrete screen allows air to circulate and prevents direct exposure to the sun. The external brick masonry is designed as two skins with a void between them.

Twelve-vent bricks were specially fired for the school. In contrast, the studios for sculptors and graphic artists enjoy light through large, north-facing windows. Thanks to this disposition, it never gets hot in the school – not even when it's 45 °C outside. To keep the winter cold in check, Max worked with Swiss experts, who suggested the use of geothermal heat exchangers (*puits canadiens*) for heating the school's large rooms (library, cinema, and large lecture room). Fresh air is drawn through underground pipes where the earth's passive heating properties temper it before it enters interior spaces as warmed air.

In his design, Max was influenced both by traditional Moroccan architecture and contemporary developments in the Maghreb. The traditional Moroccan "riad", an internal courtyard open to the sky, was the inspiration for the school's central courtyard. Other motifs are known from Guéliz, the first new district of Marrakech built under the French from 1913 onwards, while the brise-soleil is a feature known from European-influenced buildings of the 1950s. Since ÉSAV's construction, this approach has been characteristic of recent architecture in Marrakech.

From the beginning, the school's architectural style has been crucial to its institutional identity; it is, as it were, the base upon which the school's reputation rests. Apart from its flowing configuration, the way it is divided for practical use, and its many useful facilities, the building is simply lovely to look at. It is an inspiration to photographers, and is long remembered by those who visit it.

Die Architektur der Schule spielte von Anbeginn an eine wichtige Rolle für das Selbstverständnis der Institution, sie ist so etwas wie der Sockel, auf dem der Ruf der Schule aufbaut. Abgesehen von seiner fliessenden Anordnung, seiner praktischen Einteilung und seinen vielen nützlichen Einrichtungen ist das Schulgebäude auch einfach schön. Es inspiriert Fotografinnen und Fotografen und bleibt in der Erinnerung der Besucher haften.

    Die Schule hat sich in den vergangenen 15 Jahren weiterentwickelt. Rund 200 Studierende erhalten hier heute ihre Ausbildung. Neue Lehrgänge werden demnächst ins Angebot aufgenommen. Glücklicherweise steht uns noch immer Khalil Bennani zur Seite bei den Überlegungen zur Erweiterung des Gebäudes – getreu der Ethik des Schulkonzeptes, seiner architektonischen Ästhetik und der Ideen von Max.

    Ich bewege mich durch die Gänge, steige die Treppen hinauf und hinunter – und wenn ich den Blick hebe von meinem Bildschirm im Büro auf der dritten Etage, so blicke ich in den Garten des Clubs der benachbarten Universität mit seinen Palmen und dem Minarett einer Moschee, das sich vor dem Blau des Himmels und den verschneiten Gipfeln des Atlas abhebt. Ich liebe dieses Haus, es wirkt noch immer begeisternd auf mich. Es ist so etwas wie ein Gefährte, zu dem ich eine enge Beziehung pflege.

The school has developed in the last fifteen years. Some 200 students now receive their training here, and new courses are soon to be added to the curriculum. Fortunately, we still have the architect Khalil Bennani to advise us on expanding the building in line with Max's original principles for the school, his architectural aesthetic, and general ideas.

I walk along the school's corridors, go up and down stairs – and when I look up from my computer screen in my third-floor office, I have a view of the garden of the neighbouring University Club with its palm trees and a minaret highlighted against a sky of blue and the snowy peaks of the High Atlas. I love this building; it still has the ability to inspire me. It is something like a companion with whom I've long been intimately associated.

Skizzen, Zeichnungen und Aquarelle

Sketches, drawings, and watercolours

Die zum Teil in Skizzenbüchern unterwegs angefertigten Zeichnungen und Aquarelle tragen nur ausnahmsweise Ortsangaben und/oder ein Datum. Die Motive lassen die meisten Bilder Orten zuordnen, die Max Alioth oft und gerne aufgesucht hat: Paris, Marokko, Venedig, die Normandie und immer wieder die Jurahöhen (im Umkreis des Landhauses ‹Bilstein› in Langenbruck BL). Die folgende Auswahl ist in den 80er und 90er Jahren entstanden.

The drawings and watercolours produced on journeys, some of them in sketchbooks, only rarely indicate when and where exactly they were made. However, the depicted motifs often allow us to assign pictures to specific places that Max Alioth liked to and often visited, including Paris, Morocco, Venice, Normandy, and, time and again, the Jura heights (around the country residence "Bilstein" near Langenbruck, BL). The selection below is from the 1980s and 1990s.

Normandie 93 1994

Städte und Landschaften

Ulrike Jehle-Schulte Strathaus

Dass Architekten zeichnen, ist selbstverständlich. Dass sie den Zeichenstift jedoch ausserhalb des Berufs, auf Reisen etwa, einsetzen, ist im Zeitalter der handlichen Kleinbildkameras und der Polaroidmaschinen seltener geworden. Was noch bis zum Zweiten Weltkrieg jedem Baumeister vertraut war, das Zeichnen und Skizzieren unterwegs (man denke etwa an Hans Bernoullis berühmtes Skizzenbuch, herausgegeben von Paul Artaria und Hans Schmidt im Wepf Verlag) ging in den Jahren der Bauwut nach dem Kriege weitgehend verloren. Auch das, was Architekten in Fachzeitschriften vorstellten, war weniger ‹gezeichnet› als ‹grafisch dargestellt›.

Die Ausstellung der Zeichnungen und Skizzen des 51-jährigen Max Alioth ist ein Beispiel dafür, dass sich das Verhältnis des Architekten zur Architekturzeichnung, zum Zeichnen überhaupt, wieder gewandelt hat. Der zeichnerischen Präsentation eines Stücks Architektur wird allenthalben wieder Aufmerksamkeit geschenkt. Und gleichzeitig entdeckt man die Zeichnung des Architekten, die ‹nebenbei› entsteht, wieder neu.

Cities and landscapes

Ulrike Jehle-Schulte Strathaus

Everyone knows that architects produce sketches. However, today, in the age of compact cameras and polaroid machines, their use of pencils and crayons outside of their work, for example on journeys, has become a rather rare sight. While up to the Second World War, almost every architect would sketch and draw on travels (just think of Hans Bernoulli's famous sketchbook, published by Paul Artaria and Hans Schmid in Wepf Verlag), this just about came to an end during the years of the building boom after the war. And, what architects have presented in specialist journals since then hardly qualifies as "drawn", but rather as "graphically depicted".

    The exhibition featuring drawings and sketches by the 51-year-old Max Alioth is a good example to show how the architect's relationship to architectural drawing, to sketching in general, had changed again; incidentally it also shows that the graphic rendition of a piece of architecture was once again receiving more attention. At the same time, it provides an opportunity to rediscover the architect's drawings that he had produced in passing, so to speak.

    The selection of works shown here also reveals what makes an architectural drawing so valuable. Basically, it's all about spatial plasticity: how, from a distance, the cuboid forms of houses seem to melt into the landscape, or how the volumes of houses mark off a street and thus create space. There are no architectural details, no documentations of buildings, these are integral parts of earlier sketchbooks. Rather, Alioth's drawings reveal an almost sculptural interest in the stereometric patterns of a given topography. This is achieved by "pictures" that are composed of almost handwritten, craquelure-like figures or layers of small parallel pencil strokes. The drawings were created immediately in a landscape or in a town. They describe a given location in all its individuality despite a depiction's overall tendency of reduction. Yet, the drawings, which evolved alongside his professional work, are by implication

Die Auswahl der vorgestellten Arbeiten lässt die Qualitäten der Architekturzeichnung erkennen. Es geht grundsätzlich um Räumlich-Plastisches: wie die Kuben der Häuser aus der Ferne sich in die Landschaft einfügen, wie die Volumen von Gebäuden eine Strasse begrenzen und dadurch Raum schaffen. Es finden sich keine Architektur-Details, es gibt keine Bauaufnahme, diese sind fester Bestandteil früherer Skizzenbücher. Es steckt vielmehr ein fast bildhauerisches Interesse an stereometrischen Grundmustern der Topografie hinter Alioths Skizzen. Der Eindruck wird erreicht mit ‹Bildern›, die aufgebaut sind aus geschrieben wirkenden Craquelée-Figuren oder gefügt aus kleinen parallelen Strichlagen. Die Blätter entstehen direkt in der Landschaft oder in der Stadt. Sie bezeichnen einen Ort in seiner Individualität, trotz der verallgemeinernden Reduktion der Darstellung. Die Zeichnungen, die neben dem Beruf einherlaufen, sind mittelbar doch eng mit der Arbeit des Entwerfens verwandt. Da wird mit zweidimensionalen Mitteln auf Plänen versucht, Raum zu schaffen, dort wird das Erlebnis des Dreidimensionalen auf die Fläche gebracht – ein reziprokes Verhältnis also.

closely linked with the process of designing. On the one hand, two-dimensional means are used to create sculptural space on plans, on the other, the experience of three-dimensionality is conveyed to a surface – evidently a reciprocal relationship.

Ulrike Jehle-Schulte Strathaus, on the exhibition *Max Alioth Zeichnungen* at the gallery "zem Specht", 1981

Werkverzeichnis Catalogue of works

(1) **Haus im Rebberg**
Unterer Rebbergweg 124, Reinach
1961
Max Alioth
Lit. Werk 51 (1964), S. 175–177;
Reinach, Baukultur entdecken.
Schweizer Heimatschutz (Hg.), 2005

(1)

Kantonsschule Olten
Wettbewerbsprojekt (Ankauf)
Olten, Hardwald
1962/1963
Max Alioth

Gesamtüberbauung Sternenfeld, Birsfelden
Wettbewerbsprojekt (3. Preis)
Birsfelden, Sternenfeld
1963
Max Alioth

Schulhaus Erlimatt, Pratteln
Wettbewerbsprojekt (5. Preis)
Pratteln, Erliweg 12
1963
Max Alioth

(3)

Schauspielhaus Zürich
Wettbewerbsprojekt
Zürich, Heimplatz
1963/1964
Max Alioth

Primarschulhaus Bützenen, Sissach
Wettbewerbsprojekt (5. Preis)
Sissach, Bischofsteinweg 13
1964
Max Alioth

Einfamilienhaus Dr. S. Schmid
Biel-Benken
1969
Büro Alioth und Remund

Gymnasium Münchenstein
Wettbewerbsprojekt (Ankauf)
Münchenstein, Baselstrasse 33
1969
Büro Alioth und Remund

(5)

(2) Terrassensiedlung Sodacker
Pratteln, Sodackerstrasse
1969
Büro Alioth und Remund
Ingenieure E. und A. Schmidt, Basel
Gartenarchitekt P. Fisch, Pratteln
Lit. Werk 58 (1971), S. 462, 463

(2)

(3) Wohnhaus Dr. R. Kreyden
Umbauten, Ergänzungen
Reinach, Bruggstrasse 105
1969/1970, 1984 (?)
Büro Alioth und Remund

Überbauung Schlachthofareal Basel
Wettbewerbsprojekt (Ankauf)
Basel, Elsässerstrasse
1970
Büro Alioth und Remund

Alterssiedlung Pilatusstrasse
1. Preis im Wettbewerb
Basel, Pilatusstrasse 44
1971
Büro Alioth und Remund
Ausführung durch R. und H. Toffol
Bauherrschaft Genossenschaftsverband
Gotthelf-Iselin-Quartier

(4) Clubhaus des Casino-Tennis-Clubs
Basel, Emanuel Büchel-Strasse 70
1971/1972
Büro Alioth und Remund

Überbauung Kasernenareal Basel
Wettbewerbsprojckt (Ankauf)
Basel, Klingental
1972
Büro Alioth und Remund

(4)

(5) Altershotel Dalbehof
Basel, Kapellenstrasse 17
Erbaut in zwei Etappen 1972–1974
und 1983/1984
Büro Alioth und Remund
Innenausbau Richard Hersberger
Bauherrschaft Sevogel-Stiftung und
Christoph Merian Stiftung
Umbauten und Renovation 2013
durch sabarchitekten Basel
Lit. Werk 62 (1975), S. 670/671;
Ulrike Jehle-Schulte Strathaus:
Bauten im 20. Jahrhundert. Basel
1977, S. 54

⑥ Einfamilienhaus M. Breitschmid-Alioth
Binningen, Im Baumgarten 5
Büro Alioth und Remund

Weekend-Haus Dr. A. Zschokke
Himmelried
Büro Alioth und Remund

Thomas Platter-Haus
Renovation unter Aufsicht der Basler
Denkmalpflege, Bauleitung
Basel, Gundeldingerstrasse 280
1972–1974
Büro Alioth und Remund
Lit. Rudolf Suter: Die Odyssee
des Thomas Platter-Hauses, in:
Basler Stadtbuch 1974, S. 197–204

⑦

Haus im Klingental
Umbau, Renovation
Basel, Klingental 15
1973
Büro Alioth und Remund

Mehrfamilienhaus
Basel, Pfeffingerstrasse 48/50
1976
Büro Alioth und Remund
Bauingenieur Leon Goldberg
Bauherrschaft Pensions-, Witwen- und
Waisenkasse des Basler Staatspersonals
Auszeichnung Guter Bauten Kanton
Basel-Stadt 1980
Lit. Ulrike Jehle-Schulte Strathaus:
Bauten im 20. Jahrhundert. Basel 1977, S. 58

⑦ Bürohaus Sugro AG
Anbau und Renovation
Basel, Sevogelstrasse 21
1978
Büro Alioth und Remund
(Villa ‹Pfeffingerhof› von Fritz Stehlin,
 erbaut 1903)
Bauherrschaft Sugro AG,
Rohstoffhandelsfirma
Auszeichnung: Heimatschutz Basel,
Bautenprämierung 1979

⑨

Einfamilienhaus Eicher
Münchenstein,
Gutenbergstrasse 25
1978
Büro Alioth und Remund
umgebaut und aufgestockt durch
Stephan Eicher 2017

⑥

⑧

Überbauung Rosshof Basel
Wettbewerbsprojekt
Basel, Petersgraben,
Rosshofgasse
1979
Büro Alioth und Remund

⑧ Mehrfamilienhaus
Basel, Hardstrasse 54
1979/1980
Büro Alioth und Remund
Bauherrschaft H. Alioth-Wieland

Botanisches Institut der Universität
Wettbewerbsprojekt (1. Preis, nicht
ausgeführt nach Programmänderung)
Basel, Schönbeinstrasse 6
1981
Büro Alioth und Remund

Lit. Baudepartement Basel-Stadt (Hg.):
Projekte für Basel, 1979–1983.
Basel 1983, S. 59–65

⑨ Antikenmuseum Basel und Sammlung Ludwig
Umbau und Erweiterung
Basel, St. Alban-Graben 5 und 7
1984–1988
Büro Alioth und Remund
Ausbau des Ägyptensaals unter dem Hof
1999–2001
Büro Alioth Langlotz Stalder Buol
Bauherrschaft Hochbau- und Planungsamt
Basel-Stadt, Antikenmuseum und Sammlung
Ludwig

Lit. Werk, Bauen und Wohnen 68 (1981), S. 42;
Hochbauamt Basel-Stadt: Projekte für Basel,
Architektur-Wettbewerbe 1979-1983. Basel 1983, S. 39 46;
Antikenmuseum Basel und Sammlung Ludwig und
Architekturmuseum in Basel (Hg.):
Die Gebäude des Antikenmuseums.
Basel 1990

Mehrfamilienhaus
Basel, Missionsstrasse 34
1988
Büro Alioth und Remund
Bauherrschaft H. Reinhardt-Kummer

Bürohaus Intercontainer
Renovation und Erweiterung
Basel, Margarethenstrasse 38
1990/1991
Büro Alioth und Remund, mit
Susanna Biedermann
Bauherrschaft Intercontainer AG

Auszeichnung: Heimatschutz Basel,
Bautenprämierung 1991/1992

Lit. Faces Journal d'Architectures
No 16, 1990, S. 12, 13

(10) Haus für zwei
Basel, Angensteinerstrasse 35
1985/1986
Bauherr Max Alioth in Zusammenarbeit
mit Susanna Biedermann

Schul- und Förderzentrum
‹Zur Hoffnung›
Wettbewerbsprojekt
Riehen, Wenkenstrasse 3
1995
Büro Alioth, Stalder, Buol

(11) Kulturzentrum Dar Bellarj
Umbau und Restaurierung eines
ehemaligen Storchenspitals
Marrakesch
1999
Bauherrschaft Stiftung Dar Bellarj,
gegründet 1998 von Max Alioth und
Susanna Biedermann
Umbau eines historischen Hofhauses in
der Medina mit Ausstellungsräumen und
Ateliers zur Vermittlung und Förderung
der marokkanischen Kultur

Lit. Max Alioth, Beat Keusch: Susanna Biedermann:
Sehen lernen. Bern/Paris 2010; Annemarie Monteil:
Kulturzentrum in Marrakesch. Die Schule des
Schauens, in: Basler Zeitung, 11. August 2010

Geographisches Institut
der Universität Basel
Basel, Klingelbergstrasse 27
2002
Büro Alioth, Langlotz, Stalder, Buol

(12) École Supérieure des Arts Visuels
Marrakesch
2005–2007
Max Alioth in Zusammenarbeit mit
Susanna Biedermann und Khalil Bennani
Bauherrschaft Stiftung Dar Bellarj,
gegründet 1999 von Max Alioth und
Susanna Biedermann

Lit. Max Alioth, Beat Keusch: Susanna Biedermann:
Sehen lernen. Bern/Paris 2010; Annemarie Monteil:
Kulturzentrum in Marrakesch, Die Schule des
Schauens, in: Basler Zeitung, 11. August 2010; Beat
Stauffer: Afrikas beste Filmschule wurzelt in Basel.
Ein Schweizer Ehepaar hat in Marokko eine Oase
für das Kino geschaffen, in: Neue Zürcher Zeitung,
15. Juni 2020

Ausstellungen / Exhibitions:
‹Max Alioth Zeichnungen› Galerie ‹zem Specht›, Basel 1981; ‹Que des rêves continuent ...›, Zeichnungen von Max Alioth und Susanna Biedermann, Fondation Dar Bellarj, Marrakesch 2011

Beiträge / Contributions:
Max Alioth: Architektur-Wettbewerb, Beitrag zur Entwicklung, in: Hochbauamt Basel-Stadt: Projekte für Basel, Architektur-Wettbewerbe 1979–1983. Basel 1983, S. 47, 48

Bürogemeinschaften / Office partnerships:
Max Alioth führte sein Architekturbüro zunächst allein, dann als Büro ‹Alioth und Remund› 1968–1995 mit Urs Remund (1928–2012); gelegentliche Zusammenarbeit mit den Architekturbüros Nees & Beutler und Bischoff & Rüegg. Nach dem Ausscheiden von Remund formierte sich das Büro neu unter dem Namen ‹Alioth Langlotz Stalder Buol›

Das Werkverzeichnis basiert auf der Auswahl von Ulrike Jehle-Schulte Strathaus 2010, auf dem Fotoverzeichnis im Büro-Archiv im Klingental 15, Basel (verantwortlich Paul Langlotz) und auf Literaturrecherchen.

Ulrike Jehle-Schulte Strathaus
ist Kunsthistorikerin und Publizistin. 1980 Mitautorin des ersten kritischen Überblicks über die Architektur von 1940–1980 für den Propyläen-Band ‹Kunst der Gegenwart›; 1980–1986 Redaktorin der Zeitschrift ‹Werk, bauen + wohnen›; 1984–2006 leitete sie das von ihr mitbegründete Architekturmuseum Basel (heute S AM Schweizerisches Architekturmuseum); langjährige Lehrtätigkeit an der Universität Basel. / is an art historian and publicist; 1980 co-author of the first critical review of the architecture between 1940 and 1980 for the volume *Kunst der Gegenwart*, Propyläen Verlag; 1980–1986 editor of the journal *Werk, bauen + wohnen*; 1984–2006 head of the Architecture Museum Basel (now S AM Swiss Architecture Museum), which she co-founded; lecturer at the University of Basel for many years.

Beat Keusch
führt seit 1992 sein eigenes Grafik Design Studio BKVK in Basel. Davor war er, nach seiner Ausbildung zum Grafiker, in den Basler Agenturen GGK und Stalder & Suter tätig. / has managed his own graphic design studio, BKVK, in Basel since 1992. Prior to that, after training as a graphic designer, he worked for the Basel agencies GGK and Stalder & Suter.

Roger Diener
ist Architekt (Diener & Diener Architekten, Basel) und war Gastdozent an der Harvard University, USA (1989/1990), Professor an der EPFL Lausanne und der ETH Zürich (Studio Basel Contemporary City Institute, 1999–2015). Mitglied im Landesdenkmalrat Berlin (2005–2013); seit 2013 in der Kommission für Denkmalpflege der Eidgenossenschaft und seit 2018 in der Kommission für Denkmalpflege der Stadt Zürich. 2002 Grande Médaille d'Or d'Architecture Paris, 2009 Prix Meret Oppenheim, 2011 Heinrich Tessenow Medaille, 2019 der Kulturpreis der Stadt Basel. 2019 Ehrendoktor der Bauhaus-Universität Weimar. / is an architect (Diener & Diener Architekten, Basel) and was visiting professor at Harvard University, USA (1989/1990); professor at EPFL Lausanne and ETH Zurich (Studio Basel Contemporary City Institute, 1999–2015). Member of the Council of State Monuments Berlin (2005–2013), since 2013 member of the Swiss Federal Commission on the Preservation of Historical Monuments, and since 2018 member of the Zurich Commission on the Preservation of Historical Monuments. 2002 Grande Médaille d'Or d'Architecture Paris; 2009 Prix Meret Oppenheim; 2011 Heinrich Tessenow Award, 2019 Cultural Award of the City of Basel. 2019 Honorary Fellow of the Bauhaus University Weimar.

Vincent Melilli
hat in Paris Kinos instand gesetzt und wiedereröffnet, war Direktor der Französischen Institute in Marrakesch und London, hat die École Supérieure des Arts Visuels de Marrakech mitbegründet und war deren Direktor bis Dezember 2021. / restored and reopened cinemas in Paris, was director of the French Institutes in Marrakech and London, and co-founded the École Supérieure des Arts Visuels de Marrakech, which he headed until December 2021.

Andreas Ruby
ist Architekturkritiker, Publizist, Buchverleger und Kurator. Nach seinem Studium der Kunstgeschichte war er zunächst als freier Architekturkritiker tätig, bevor er 2008 zusammen mit Ilka Ruby den Architekturbuchverlag Ruby Press gründete. Seit 2016 ist er Direktor des S AM Schweizerisches Architekturmuseum in Basel. / is an architectural critic, writer, publisher, and curator. After studying Art History, he worked as a freelance architectural critic before establishing the architectural publishing house Ruby Press together with Ilka Ruby in 2008. He has been director of the S AM Swiss Architecture Museum in Basel since 2016.

Fotonachweis / Photo credits:
Claire Niggli: 10, 66
Susana Bruell: 12 oben / above
Serge Hasenböhler: 34–44
Leonardo Bezzola: 46–52, 164 ⑤
Christian Vogt: 64–65, 69–86, 168 ⑩
Catherine Hilal: 88–89, 110, 115
Hassan Nadim: 93, 169 ⑪
Alf Dietrich: 95
Beat Keusch: 104–105, 116–119, 169 ⑫
Younes Belbahri: 113 oben / above
Mohcine Kamal: 114 oben / above
Christian Baur: 166 ⑦
Christian Lichtenberg: 166 ⑨
Arnaud Contreras: 168 ⑪

In einigen Fällen konnten die Urheber- und Abdruckrechte trotz umfangreicher Recherche nicht ermittelt werden. Viele Pläne und Fotos werden im Archiv des ehemaligen Büros Alioth Langlotz Stalder Buol Architekten im Klingental 15 in Basel aufbewahrt. / In some cases, the copyright and printing rights could not be ascertained despite extensive research. Many of the plans and photographs are still kept in the archives of the former architectural office Alioth Langlotz Stalder Buol at Klingental 15 in Basel.

Konzept / Concept:
Beat Keusch, Ulrike Jehle-Schulte Strathaus

Redaktion / Editorial work:
Dorothee Huber

Projektleitung / Project management:
Beat Keusch

Übersetzung / Translation:
Nigel Stephenson

Lektorat und Korrektorat / Copy-editing and proofreading:
Doris Tranter

Gestaltung / Graphic design:
BKVK – Sarah Wolfsberger, Ladina Ingold, Beat Keusch

Lithografie / Lithography:
Georg Sidler, Samuel Trutmann

Papier / Paper:
Napura Khepera Azur, 135 g/m. Magno Volume 1.05

Schrift / Typeface:
Suisse Works, Swiss Typefaces

Druck und Bindung / Printing and binding:
DZA Druckerei zu Altenburg

© 2022 Bernhard Spoendlin und / and
Verlag Scheidegger & Spiess AG, Zürich

© für die Texte / regarding the texts:
die Autor:innen / the authors

© für die Fotos / regarding the photographs:
die Fotograf:innen / the photographers

© für das abgebildete Plakat S. 17: S AM /
for the reproduced poster p. 17: S AM

Verlag Scheidegger & Spiess
Niederdorfstrasse 54
8001 Zürich
Schweiz / Switzerland
www.scheidegger-spiess.ch

Der Verlag Scheidegger & Spiess wird vom Bundesamt für Kultur mit einem Strukturbeitrag für die Jahre 2021–2024 unterstützt. / Scheidegger & Spiess is being supported by the Federal Office of Culture with a general subsidy for the years 2021–2024.

Alle Rechte vorbehalten; kein Teil dieses Werks darf in irgendeiner Form ohne vorherige schriftliche Genehmigung des Verlags reproduziert oder unter Verwendung elektronischer Systeme verarbeitet, vervielfältigt oder verbreitet werden. / All rights reserved; no part of this publication may be reproduced, stored in a retrieval system or transmitted in any form or by any means, electronic, mechanical, photocopying, recording, or otherwise, without the prior written consent of the publisher.

ISBN 978-3-03942-089-6

Printed in Germany

Die Herausgabe dieses Buches wurde ermöglicht durch Béatrice Spoendlin-Alioth und das S AM Schweizerisches Architekturmuseum. / Béatrice Spoendlin and the S AM Swiss Architecture Museum enabled the publication of this volume.